LEFT TO DIE

CHAPPAQUIDDICK GRAND JURY FOREMAN REVEALS EXPLOSIVE, NEVER-TOLD BEFORE INFORMATION

BY
JERRY SHAFFER
AND
LESLIE H. LELAND

Strategic Book Publishing
New York, New York

Strategic Book Publishing
An imprint of Writers Literary & Publishing Services, Inc.
845 Third Avenue, 6th Floor – 6016
New York, NY 10022
http://www.strategicbookpublishing.com

ISBN:978-1-60911-139-7

Printed in the United States of America

Book Design: Bonita S. Watson

DEDICATION

This book is dedicated to Leslie's brother and my brother-in-law, Jack Leland, a Vietnam War veteran—and to the memory of the Kopechnes: Mary Jo, the victim, and her parents Gwen and Joe, who lived all those years in sorrow, never knowing what really happened.

ACKNOWLEDGMENTS

This book could not have been written without the assistance of many people and many sources, including Phil Pankiewicz, Mary and Tony Prevett, Graeme Pentland, Senatorial Privilege by Leo Damore, The Bridge at Chappaquiddick by Jack Olsen, Death at Chappaquiddick by Richard L. and Thomas L. Tedrow, the Boston Globe, the Police Times, and various Web sites including ytedk.com as well as the support of Jim and Denise Bryan.

Also, I want to thank Sue Leland for her cordial hospitality during my visits to Martha's Vineyard, and especially thank my wife, Sher Shaffer, for putting up with my time in writing this book twice … the first time, and then the second after Hurricane Wilma destroyed my hard drive after my brilliance in not backing up and saving my original effort. She was also very well-versed on the Chappaquiddick accident, and instrumental in getting me interested in writing this book with Les Leland and providing and substantiating many of the facts. She also came up with the title for the book.

THE MAIN PEOPLE:

John B. Crimmins, part-time chauffeur for Senator Kennedy
Joseph Gargan, Senator's cousin, a lawyer
Edward M. Kennedy, Senator from Massachusetts
Raymond S. LaRosa, Kennedy campaign worker
Paul F. Markham, ex-U.S. Attorney from Massachusetts
Charles C. Tretter, Kennedy campaign aide
The "boiler room" girls, all former workers for Robert Kennedy
      Rosemary "Cricket" Keough
      Mary Jo Kopechne
      Ann "Nance"   Lyons
      Maryellen Lyons
      Esther Newburgh
      Susan Tannenbaum
Dominic James Arena, Edgartown Police Chief
Edmund S. Dinis, District Attorney
James A. Boyle, district court judge
John Farrar, head of Search and Rescue division
Christopher "Huck" Look, deputy sheriff
Walter Steele, special prosecutor
Dr. Donald R. Mills, associate medical examiner
Eugene Frieh, undertaker
Wilfred Paquet, judge for grand jury

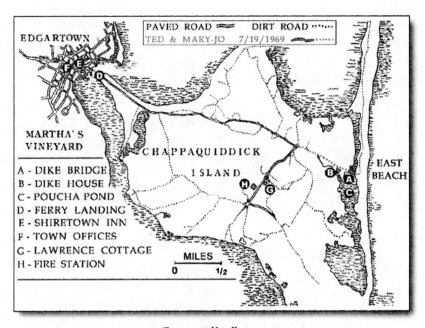

Courtesy Ytedk.com

Things you should know:

The town of Edgartown, one of six towns on Martha's Vineyard, includes a small island called Chappaquiddick.

The mainland of Edgartown is separated from Chappaquiddick by Edgartown Harbor, which is approximately five hundred feet wide. Transportation between the mainland and island is provided by ferry.

Chappaquiddick has few roads. Chappaquiddick Road begins at the ferry slip. It is a macadam-paved road, the main one on the island, with a white center line which is partially obliterated at the curve. It is approximately 20 feet wide and runs in a general easterly direction for 2.5 miles before it curves south and continues in that direction. Chappaquiddick Road is also known as Main Street, and after it curves the name changes to School Road or Schoolhouse Road.

At the curve, and continuing in an easterly direction, begins Dike Road, a dirt, sand and gravel road that runs about seven-tenths of a mile to Dike Bridge, which is right before the ocean beach. The road is 15 feet wide at the bridge.

Katama Shores Motor Inn is located about 2 miles from the ferry slip.

Shiretown Inn is about one block from the ferry landing.

Dike Bridge is a wooden structure, 10 feet 6 inches wide. The timber curbs on each side are 4 inches high and 10 inches wide. There are no other guardrails. The bridge runs at an angle of 27 degrees to the left of the road. There are no signs or artificial lights on the bridge or at its approach. It spans Poucha Pond.

Kennedy's car, a black Oldsmobile, was 18 feet long and 80 inches wide.

Poucha Pond is a saltwater tidal pond. It has a strong current where it narrows at Dike Bridge.

Cemetery Road is a single-car-width private dirt road which runs north from the junction of Chappaquiddick and Dike Roads.

The Lawrence cottage is one-half mile from the junction of Chappaquiddick and Dike Roads, approximately 3 miles from the ferry landing.

A driver leaving the Lawrence cottage and heading in a northerly direction toward the ferry landing, will see a metal sign with an arrow pointing toward the ferry landing on the east side (right side) of Chappaquiddick Road, about one-tenth of a mile before the curve.

PROLOGUE

PARTY TIME

It was a warm, balmy evening on the Island. In a rented cottage on Martha's Vineyard, it was party time. Five married gentlemen. Six young single girls. An abundance of appetizers. Cocktails flowing. Steaks sizzling on the grill. It was noisy, with conversations going on throughout the house and music blasting. Everyone was having a ball. It was fun, fun, fun.

One of the male guests decided to leave around 11:15 that night. One of the female guests asked the gentleman if he was going to the ferry. He said yes and offered her a ride. She graciously accepted.

They drove down the paved road to the ferry, a trip he had taken several times earlier that day. Suddenly, he took a hard right onto a dirt road filled with gravel. Being familiar with the area, surely he must have known this wasn't the way to the ferry. This was not the paved road that started the trip.

Continuing down the gravel dirt road at about 20 miles per hour or more for about three-quarters of a mile, he suddenly saw a bridge and water in front of him. He slammed on the brakes, but couldn't stop the car in time. They crashed through the guard rail into the water. The car sank.

Miraculously, he got out of the car and swam to the surface. She was trapped in the car. He made numerous attempts to dive into the water down to the car to save her, but to no avail. He continued these attempts until he was exhausted and couldn't continue.

He rested on the bank for awhile before starting his trek back to the house to get help. As he started to walk, he passed a house with a light on outside. However, he didn't notice it. Across the street, there was another house with a light on in the children's room. He didn't notice that either. He also passed the volunteer fire house.

He arrived back at the party house and summoned his two friends. He told them what had happened, but asked they not tell anyone else at the party. They all drove to the site of the accident. His two friends jumped into the water and tried to save the lady passenger. He sat on the bank, too exhausted to join in the effort. As hard as they tried, they were unable to rescue her.

Finally, after some time, his two friends gave up the search. The three got back in the car and headed for the ferry dock. The two who attempted the rescue told their friend he must immediately report the accident to the police. He said he would take care of it. Since the ferry was not there, he jumped in the water and swam to the other side. Amazing, for a man too exhausted to continue trying to reach his passenger, or assist his friends in their efforts to save the girl.

SEQUENCE OF EVENTS:

July 18–19, 1969: Senator Ted Kennedy drives off Dike Bridge. Mary Jo Kopechne is killed.

July 19: Senator gives statement of accident to police.

July 22: Mary Jo is buried.

July 25: Kennedy pleads guilty to leaving the scene of an accident. Kennedy gives televised speech.

July 31: District Attorney Edmund S. Dinis requests inquest into the death of Mary Jo.

August 8: Judge Boyle sets inquest date of September 3. (The inquest is eventually delayed.)

October 30: The Massachusetts Supreme Judicial Court bars the press and public from the inquest, and orders all documents impounded until after all possible prosecution against Senator Kennedy is ended.

December 11: Judge Boyle sets January 5, 1970, as the date for the inquest.

January 5–8, 1970: Senator Kennedy and twenty-six other witnesses testify at inquest.

March 17: Leslie Leland, foreman of the grand jury, requests that a special session be reconvened.

March 26: Chief Justice Joseph G. Tauro of the Superior Court calls for a special session of the court to convene on April 6 for the grand jury to hear evidence.

April 6–7: The grand jury calls four witnesses and returns no indictments. D.A. Dinis declares the case is closed, and documents can now be made public.

April 29: Documents of inquest are released to the public.

TABLE OF CONTENTS

Chapter 1

Introduction

Those of you who know the incident may still recall the bewilderment and controversy surrounding this infamous automobile accident. For those of you who are too young to remember, what we briefly described was the event on Chappaquiddick Island. The man was Senator Edward Moore (Ted) Kennedy. The woman was Mary Jo Kopechne. Let's go back to bring you up-to-date on the events leading up to this tragedy and the alleged cover-up ... possibly the greatest of all time.

It was an incident that totally consumed the public's curiosity and one that was covered worldwide by newspapers, radio and television stations. Now, some 40 years later, Leslie (Les) Leland, the grand jury foreman who led the investigation, reveals his story. The grand jury was stymied in its pursuit of the truth into Mary Jo Kopechne's death at Chappaquiddick. It is Leland's hope that both the general public and historians will gain further insight into the events that occurred during the months of lengthy, but futile, investigation. Readers will discover how Leland became a major player in the district court judge's final decision, and how his lack of courtroom expertise stymied him and the other jurors time and time again. This tragedy tore apart a family, and ruined one man's chances of becoming president of the United States.

Several books, especially Leo Damore's *Senatorial Privilege: The Chappaquiddick Cover-Up*, have already probed deeply into this controversy. *Left to Die* summarizes those findings and adds important information. Leland, for example, describes his clandestine meeting before the grand jury's inquiry, which left him "shaken and confused." He explains how Leslie's Drug Store on Main Street in Vineyard Haven became the central hotbed of rumors, innuendos and media frenzy. He also relates his meetings with Leo Damore, and how Damore's book and subsequent divorce led to the author's suicide. *Left to Die* is a story finally told by the one person who might have changed the course of history.

The weekend of July 18, 1969, was the date of the annual Edgartown Sailing Regatta, which Kennedy regularly participated in. In addition, a party was planned that evening for six of the "Boiler Room" girls who had worked for Robert Kennedy, and five friends and relatives of the Senator. The girls at the party were Rosemary "Cricket" Keough, Maryellen Lyons, Nance Lyons, Esther Newburgh, Susan Tannenbaum, and, of course, Mary Jo. The men included Jack Crimmins, Joe Gargan, Ray LaRosa, Paul Markham, and Charles Tretter.

Kennedy reportedly arrived at Martha's Vineyard Island, off the coast of Cape Cod, Massachusetts early in the afternoon of July 18. He had left the mainland onboard the *Ferry Islander*, and arrived in Vineyard Haven where his part-time chauffeur, Jack Crimmins, met him. They drove to Edgartown, where they boarded a ferry called *On Time* for a short hop across the harbor to an island affectionately called Chappy, short for Chappaquiddick.

The Senator went to the Lawrence Cottage, which he rented, to change into a bathing suit to join the girls at the beach. To get to the beach, Crimmins drove him down a paved highway named School Road, and took a hard right onto Dike Road, an unpaved dirt road covered with gravel. They drove over the Dike Bridge and Poucha Pond to the beach. After about an hour, they all left the beach and went back to Edgartown to participate in the Regatta.

After the Regatta, Kennedy and some of the crew from his boat *Victura*, along with Stan Moore, an automobile dealer from Cape Cod, who had crewed aboard the *Uncle Benny*, joined Ross

Richards on his winning boat *Bettawin*. They all had drinks and discussed the race. Gargan stayed behind to lower the sails and batten down the hatches on *Victura*. Markham returned to his hotel room, because he injured his leg during the race.

Moore and Kennedy each had three drinks while on the *Bettawin*. Moore is said to have remembered it specifically because they were both drinking rum and Coke. When questioned by authorities, Moore refused to comment on Kennedy's alcoholic intake. Later, Moore supposedly admitted that "Ted had three rum and Cokes in about twenty minutes, but I didn't think it was anybody's business."

Later, Gargan joined the others on board, but by that time Kennedy was ready to leave. Kennedy and Gargan went back to the Shiretown Inn, where Gargan ordered a six-pack of Heinekens. Jack Crimmins was already there. Markham had checked out because he was planning to stay the night at the party cottage.

At about 7:00 p.m., Crimmins drove Kennedy to the ferry, which they took over to Chappaquiddick. Nobody was at the cottage when they arrived, so Kennedy took a hot bath and Crimmins prepared him a rum and Coke.

Ray LaRosa picked up the girls at their motel and drove them to the ferry. He parked the car at the Shiretown Inn and walked back to the dock. They all took the ferry over to Chappy and were met by Gargan, who drove them to the cottage in the rented white Valiant.

The party took place at the Lawrence Cottage on Chappaquiddick. Appetizers were served. And, according to several participants, there was plenty of liquor of all types available. Even though everyone stated that they had only one or two drinks, the empty bottles found after the party indicate that if their statements were true, the liquor must have evaporated. Gargan, who was not feeling well, did not drink that night. He did reportedly observe, "Some people at the party had had quite a few, no question. Frankly, everybody was a little bombed, except for LaRosa, who doesn't drink."

Steaks were grilled and served during the evening's festivities. The party was loud and noisy. A neighboring couple said the noise was deafening, with loud voices and louder music. Foster Silva, the fire captain, lived about 100 yards from the Lawrence cottage. He had a vivid memory of the party. He said he watched TV until about 10:00 p.m., when his dogs started barking constantly. He went out to quiet them, and saw two cars at the Lawrence cottage.

"There was a lot of singing and laughing coming from the house. I would say it was just a normal cocktail party. They were damned loud, though," said Silva.

He said he went to bed about midnight, but couldn't fall asleep because of all the noise coming from the neighboring cottage. Silva thought the partygoers were inconsiderate in not keeping the noise down after 11:00 p.m.

"By 1:00 a.m., I was pretty damn well fed up with the whole thing. It was a damn farce at that hour of the morning. If they had kept it up any longer, I would have called the police," Silva said.

Silva's son-in-law seconded the fire captain's statement, describing the party as "one of those loud, noisy brawls put on by summer people. There was yelling, music, and general sounds of hell-raising." About 1:30 in the morning, the noise carried on. "You could still hear people talking, but the noise level was not so bad. It was still going on when I went to bed at 2:30 a.m."

Sometime, reportedly about 11:15 that night, Senator Kennedy decided to leave the party and return to his room at the Shiretown Inn on Edgartown. At the time he was talking to Mary Jo, who said she wasn't feeling well. She asked if he would mind driving her. They purportedly left for the ferry in that time frame. Kennedy did not ask Crimmins to drive them, as he usually did. In fact, he insisted that he drive, even though Crimmins objected. Kennedy drove with Mary Jo beside him. He left the cottage and started down School Road, the paved road. Then, suddenly, he made a hard right onto Dike Road, the bumpy, dirt road filled with gravel. Driving too fast for the conditions, he couldn't stop the car as it plunged off the bridge and submerged into Poucha Pond.

Interestingly, less than a year before this accident, the Army Core of Engineers hired the New England Dredge and Dock Company, of Falmouth, Massachusetts, to deepen waterways for boat traffic and use the sand to build beaches on Cape Cod and the islands. They dredged the area from a depth of 3 feet to 15 feet.

The dredge captain was John T. Dunn, known as Captain Jack. He and the entire crew were Newfoundlanders. When working on the islands, they would work for a week straight, staying on the island, and then the Captain and crew would be off for three days before returning for another week's work.

Of course, without this dredging, the accident undoubtedly would not have caused the death of Mary Jo.

As stated earlier, the Senator said he somehow escaped from the car and tried numerous times to dive down and save Mary Jo. He was unsuccessful. Completely exhausted, he rested on the bank before starting back to the cottage to get help.

When he got back, he got into the white Valiant parked outside. He saw Ray LaRosa, a veteran campaign worker, and told him to get Joe Gargan, Kennedy's cousin and co-host of the party. After Gargan got in the car, Kennedy asked LaRosa to get Paul Markham, a very close friend, as well.

Kennedy then described what happened. They drove to the scene of the accident, where Gargan and Markham jumped into the water and dove down trying to get to Mary Jo. They were unsuccessful after many attempts. Kennedy remained on the bank, too exhausted to help.

Kennedy asked to be taken back to the Chappy ferry so he could return to his room at the Shiretown Inn. On the way, both Gargan and Markham insisted that Ted report the accident to the police immediately. But the Senator did not want to report it. Kennedy continually suggested possible alternative statements that would admonish him of any guilt, but both Gargan and Markham refused to accept any of these contrived statements. They continued to insist that he report the accident immediately and accurately. Finally, he agreed and said he would take care of it. When they got to the ferry dock, amidst much conversation, Kennedy suddenly jumped into the water and started swimming across to Edgartown. Gargan and Markham watched until they saw him reach the other side.

When he arrived at Edgartown, Kennedy went back to his room and dressed in a jacket and slacks. He then went outside and ran into a room clerk named Russell Peachey, while standing at the bottom of the stairway leading up to his room on the second floor.

Peachey asked the Senator, "May I help you in any way?

Kennedy told him he had been bothered by noises coming from a party next door. He also couldn't find his watch, and asked Peachey what time it was.

Peachey looked through a window in his office and saw the clock that showed the time as 2:25 a.m. He then asked the Senator, "Is there anything else I can do to help you?"

"Thank you, no," said Kennedy, and he returned to his room.

Peachey later said of his encounter with Kennedy, "He didn't look to me like a man who had come downstairs to complain about noise. He was just standing there. He was fully dressed. I think he was wearing a jacket and slacks. Usually, a man who just wants to complain about noise doesn't get up and get fully dressed to do it. Especially at 2:25 in the morning."

The Senator went back to his room, slept and awoke the next morning. He showered, shaved and dressed as if nothing had happened. He met with people the next morning and went about his business. Kennedy got on the ferry to Chappaquiddick, and it was then that he was told a car had been found in Poucha Pond. When he arrived on Chappy, he made numerous phone calls to confidants and lawyers. Finally, some ten hours after the accident, he showed up at the police station. He made a written statement as follows:

"On July 18, 1969, at approximately 11:15 p.m. in Chappaquiddick, Martha's Vineyard, Massachusetts, I was driving my car on Main Street on my way to get the ferry back to Edgartown. I was unfamiliar with the road and turned right onto Dike

Road, instead of bearing hard left on Main Street. After proceeding for approximately one-half mile on Dike Road I descended a hill and came upon a narrow bridge. The car went out off the side of the bridge. There was one passenger with me, one Mary _____, a former secretary of my brother Sen. Robert Kennedy. The car turned over and sank into the water and landed with the roof resting on the bottom.

"I attempted to open the door and the window of the car but have no recollection of how I got out of the car. I came to the surface and then repeatedly dove down to the car in an attempt to see if the passenger was still in the car. I was unsuccessful in the attempt. I was exhausted and in a state of shock.

"I recall walking back to where my friends were eating. There was a car parked in front of the cottage and I climbed into the back seat. I then asked for someone to bring me back to Edgartown. I remember walking around for a period and then going back to my hotel room. When I fully realized what had happened this morning, I immediately contacted the police."

Now, let's briefly dissect this statement. To start with, he never mentioned the party or his participation in it, only that he walked back to where his friends were eating. Secondly, he was not unfamiliar with the road. He had been sailing in the Regatta for years. He had driven the road several times that day. He did not immediately contact the police. As Bernie Flynn, a state police detective lieutenant, said after hearing the statement, "Personally, I thought it was bullshit." Even Kennedy supporters knew it could not have been a mistake. Nobody in condition to drive a car could confuse a dirt road with a macadam one. Also, he didn't even state Mary Jo Kopechne's full name.

Then, he stated he turned right onto Dike Road instead of bearing hard left on Main Street. The only problem is that there is no hard left, as Main Street--a paved street--continues with a gradual left curve, while Dike Road is a dirt road filled with gravel, is extremely bumpy, and requires a very sharp 90-degree turn. How anyone could continue down a dirt road and not know that it is not the continuation of a paved road is beyond comprehension. Not to mention the fact that he had to make a very sharp, hard right to get onto the dirt road, a turn that could only be made, without skidding, traveling at a very, very slow pace.

Descending a hill is also questionable, as there is no real hill or anything anyone might consider a hill.

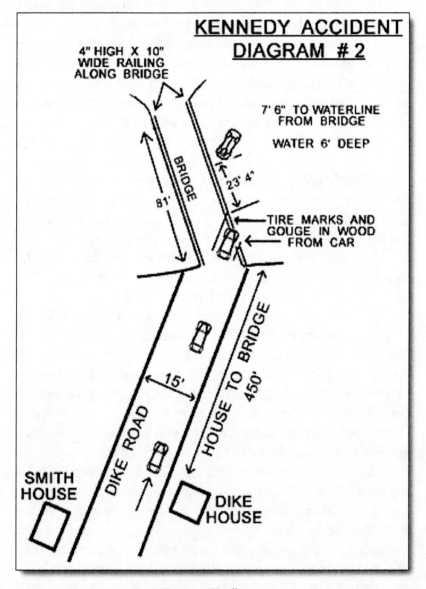

Courtesy Ytedk.com

He has no recollection of how he got out of the car, although as we go further into the happenings, you will notice the discrepancies in his stories about the car and the condition of the car when it was brought to the surface.

On his walk back to the cottage, he doesn't recall seeing the porch light or the light in the children's room, both of which were certainly visible on a pitch-black night. Also interesting is the statement of his unfamiliarity with the area, despite his ability to walk right back to the cottage.

Finally, he fails to mention the efforts of Markham and Gargan to save Ms. Kopechne. He doesn't say a word about the party at the cottage. And, of course, we must assume that 10 hours later is the equivalent of immediately contacting the police.

Chief Arena never questioned Kennedy and had only one piece of evidence, the written statement. He began writing a traffic violation based on Chapter 90, Section 24 which reads: "Any operator of a vehicle who, without stopping and making known his name, residence, and the registration number of his motor vehicle, goes away after knowingly colliding with, or otherwise causing injury to any person, shall be punished by imprisonment for not less than twenty days or more than two years."

Arena asked Kennedy for his driver's license, but the Senator did not have one with him. According to Leo Damore's book, *Senatorial Privilege,* the chief then called the Oak Bluffs Registry Office to get the information and was told that they would get back to him.

Kennedy's office could not find the Senator's license in Washington, and an administrative aide contacted Registry Officer George Kennedy and reported the missing license. The inspector called the Boston office to request a license check for the Senator.

The following is what we have been told happened in the license search. Joseph Mellino, the registry inspector in Boston who received the call, went into the file room to check the license cards, which are kept in alphabetical order. He found that the license had expired on February 22, 1969, and had not been renewed.

Inspector Kennedy then ordered Mellino to pull the license card, put it together with the car's registration, and either give it to Registrar Richard McLaughlin or place it on his desk.

Inspector Kennedy was very disturbed to learn that the Senator had not only left the scene of an accident, but also was driving on an expired license. The inspector then called Joe Greelish, the regional head of motor vehicles for southeastern Massachusetts. Greelish told the inspector not to give information about the expired license to anyone, including Chief Arena. Kennedy knew that concealing such information from investigating authorities was unusual, but he still stalled in providing the data.

Greelish contacted Registrar McLaughlin, told him about the expired license, and said that he would personally take over the case "so it doesn't get screwed up."

Later that evening, Joe Greelish contacted assistant district attorney Jimmy Smith, telling him that the Senator's license had expired, but this information had been concealed and now the "problem has been taken care of."

On Sunday, July 20, Greelish provided Chief Arena with Senator Kennedy's driver's license information, indicating that it was valid until February 22, 1971. Amazing, how these problems are handled.

When Arena received this information, he completed his citation for the traffic accident. He could only charge the Senator with leaving the scene of an accident after causing personal injury. Since he didn't know about the expired license, and because there was no provable evidence that the Senator was driving under the influence of liquor, the chief had no alternative. He said, "We don't and probably will not have a case of negligent driving in the criminal sense."

The chief described the accident scene: "Car #1 being operated East on Dike Road at unknown rate of speed—this roadway is a dirt road approximately 2 car widths wide—operator descended a bit on roadway and came to a narrow (10'6" wide) bridge which went off to the left from the roadway at about a 25 - 30 degree angle. Car 1 was unable to stop upon entering the bridge and hit the small running rail (approx. 4" high x 10' wide), which ran along sides of the bridge. The car went off the bridge and turned over landing in the water."

CHAPTER 2

QUESTIONS WITHOUT ANSWERS

Some very interesting happenings must have made everyone question the Senator's statement. There was Christopher "Huck" Look, a deputy sheriff on duty that night. He reported seeing the car, or one just like it, at the corner about 12:45 a.m. Though he didn't remember the license number for certain, he knew certain numbers, like L7 and 7, that were the same as the car in the accident. (The actual license number was L78-207.) When he saw the car pulled out of the water, he said, "This is the same car I saw last night." After being told that it was Senator Ted Kennedy's car, Look facetiously said, "I didn't see a thing."

Dominick James Arena, the Edgartown Police Chief, said upon examining the car, "The driver of the car would have to have taken a really hard blow to the head, because the windshield on the driver's side was badly smashed in." Upon seeing Kennedy the morning after the accident, he couldn't reconcile Kennedy's appearance with the driver of a car in such an accident. Further, after looking at the bridge, he could not find skid marks. They were more like scuff marks, caused by sliding rather than skidding on the side rails of the bridge.

Mrs. Sylvia Malm, who owned the cottage about 400 feet from the pond, reported hearing a car going faster than usual about midnight. John Farrar, who was head of the Search and Rescue Division of the Edgartown Volunteer Fire Department, dove in with his scuba gear to see if rescue was possible. He said, after he found the car and its occupant, that the car was facing in the opposite direction it had been traveling. Only speed could account for such aerial maneuvers. "The car must have been going at a pretty good clip to land almost in the middle of the channel."

Dr. Donald R. Mills, an associate medical examiner, was called to the scene of the accident. He examined the body and was convinced that drowning was the cause of death. There were calls for an autopsy, but Mills insisted that drowning was the cause. George Killen, a detective lieutenant with the state police, was contacted about the possibility of an autopsy. Dr. Mills wanted to know what he should do. Killen sent a message through one of his officers that if Mills was certain about his diagnosis, and there was no sign of foul play, there was no need for an autopsy.

Eugene Frieh, an undertaker on Martha's Vineyard, doubted Mills' report. The lack of water evacuated from the body was unusual in a drowning case. He thought the cause of death might have been suffocation. When he suggested that Mills change his finding, the doctor said "he didn't want to cause any problem" and would not order an autopsy. Frieh wanted an autopsy because of the type of accident, the people involved, and the insurance companies hounding officials over double indemnity claims.

Farrar, seeing the rear passenger window blown out, stated that if Kopechne had been killed or knocked unconscious by the impact of the crash, she would have been prone, sinking to the bottom or floating on top. Instead, she was definitely holding herself in a position to breathe the last remaining air that had to be trapped in the car.

Nevertheless, there was no autopsy, and Killen had no one to blame but himself.

CHAPTER 3

THE SENATOR SAYS HE'S SORRY . . . OR DOES HE?

In Massachusetts, the law states that when a person is killed in an accident, the prosecution must bring an action for criminal manslaughter. There must be a hearing.

Chief Arena knew that a manslaughter charge was mandatory. Walter Steele, the special prosecutor, knew that driving off the bridge was a case of negligence, but knowing who the driver was made him reluctant to make this charge to Arena. And Arena did not want to make such a serious charge against the Senator.

In the end, Kennedy pleaded guilty to operating a motor vehicle upon a public way and leaving, after knowingly causing injury, without stopping and making known his name, residence and the license number of his motor vehicle. His mandatory sentence was suspended. This was a very minor charge, considering what he—could have been accused of.

The Senator attended Mary Jo's funeral with his wife Joan. It's interesting to note, we understand that the only time he wore a protective collar in public was at the funeral.

After the funeral, on Friday of the week following the accident, the Senator went on TV to make his statement of the events.

"My fellow citizens:

"I have requested this opportunity to talk to you, the people of Massachusetts, about the tragedy which happened last Friday evening.

"This morning, I entered a plea of guilty to the charge of leaving the scene of an accident. Prior to my appearance in court, it would have been improper for me to comment on these matters, but tonight I am free to tell you what happened and to say what it means to me.

"On the weekend of July 18, I was on Martha's Vineyard Island participating with my nephew, Joe Kennedy, as for thirty years my family has participated in the annual Edgartown Sailing Regatta. Only reasons of health prevented my wife from accompanying me.

"On Chappaquiddick Island off Martha's Vineyard, I attended on Friday evening, July 18, a cookout I had encouraged and helped sponsor for a devoted group of Kennedy campaign secretaries. When I left the party around 11:15 p.m., I was accompanied by one of these girls, Miss Mary Jo Kopechne. Mary Jo was one of the most devoted members of the staff of Senator Robert Kennedy. She worked for him for four years and was broken up over his death. For this reason, and because she was such a gentle, kind and idealistic person, all of us tried to help her feel that she still had a home with the Kennedy family.

"There is no truth whatsoever to the widely circulated suspicions of immoral conduct that have been leveled at my behavior and hers regarding that evening. There has never been a private relationship between us of any kind. I know of nothing in Mary Jo's conduct on that or any other occasion—and the same is true of the other girls at that party—that would lend any substance to such ugly speculation about their character. Nor was I driving under the influence of liquor.

"Little over a mile away, the car that I was driving on an unlit road went off a narrow bridge which had no guard rails and was built on a left angle to the road. The car overturned into a deep pond and immediately filled with water. I remember thinking, as the cold water rushed in around my head, that I was for certain drowning. Then water entered my lungs and I actually felt a sensation of drowning, but somehow I struggled to the surface alive. I made immediate and repeated efforts to save Mary Jo by diving into the strong and murky current, but succeeded only in increasing my state of utter exhaustion and alarm.

"My conduct and conversations during the next several hours, to the extent that I can remember them, made no sense to me at all. Although my doctors inform me that I suffered a cerebral concussion as well as shock, I do not seek to escape responsibility for my actions by placing the blame either on the physical and emotional trauma brought on by the accident, or on anyone else. I regard as indefensible the fact that I did not report the accident to the police immediately.

"Instead of looking directly for a telephone after lying exhausted on the grass for an undetermined time, I walked back to the cottage where the party was being held, requested the help of two friends, Joe Gargan and Paul Markham, and directed them to return immediately to the scene with me (it then being sometime after midnight) in order to undertake a new effort to dive down and locate Miss Kopechne. Their strenuous efforts, undertaken at some risk to their own lives, also proved futile.

"All kinds of scrambled thoughts—all of them confused, some of them irrational, many of which I cannot recall, and some of which I would not have seriously entertained under normal circumstances—went through my mind during this period. They were reflected in the various inexplicable, inconsistent and inconclusive things I said and did—including such questions as whether the girl might still be alive somewhere out of that immediate area, whether some awful curse actually did hang over all the Kennedys, whether there was some justifiable reason for me to doubt what had happened and to delay my report, and whether somehow the awful weight of this incredible incident might in some way pass from my shoulders. I was overcome, I am frank to say, by a jumble of emotions—grief, fear, doubt, exhaustion, panic, confusion and shock.

"Instructing Gargan and Markham not to alarm Mary Jo's friends that night, I had them take me to the ferry crossing. The ferry having shut down for the night, I suddenly jumped into the water and impulsively swam across, nearly drowning once again in the effort, returning to my hotel around 2:00 a.m. and collapsed in my room. I remember going out at one point and saying something to the room clerk. In the morning, with my mind somewhat more lucid, I made an effort to call a family legal adviser, Burke Marshall, from a public telephone on the Chappaquiddick side of the ferry, and then belatedly reported the accident to the Martha's Vineyard police.

"Today, as mentioned, I felt morally obligated to plead guilty to the charge of leaving the scene of an accident. No words on my part can possibly express the terrible pain and suffering I feel over this tragic accident. This last week has been an agonizing one for me and for the members of my family; and the grief we feel over the loss of a wonderful friend will remain with us the rest of our lives."

Kennedy then put down his prepared speech and continued:

"These events, and the publicity and innuendo and whispers which have surrounded them, and my admission of guilt this morning, raises the question in my mind of whether my standing among the people of my state has been so impaired that I should resign my seat in the United States Senate. If at any time the citizens of Massachusetts should lack confidence in their Senator's character or his ability, with or without justification, he could not, in my opinion, adequately perform his duties, and should not continue in office.

"The people of this state—the state which sent John Quincy Adams, Daniel Webster, Charles Sumner, Henry Cabot Lodge, and John F. Kennedy to the United States Senate—are entitled to representation in that body by men who inspire their utmost confidence. For this reason, I would understand full well why some might think it right for me to resign.

"This would be a difficult decision to make. It has been seven years since my first election to the Senate. You and I share many memories. Some of them have been glorious, some have been very sad. The opportunity to work with you and serve our state has been much of what has made my life worthwhile.

"And so I ask you tonight, the people of Massachusetts, to think this through with me. In facing this decision, I seek your advice and opinion. In making it, I seek your prayers. For this is a decision that I will have finally to make on my own.

"It has been written: 'A man does what he must—in spite of personal consequences, in spite of obstacles and dangers and pressures—and that is the basis of all human morality. And whatever may be the sacrifices he faces if he follows his con-science—the loss of his friends, his fortune, his contentment, even the esteem of his fellow men—each man must decide for himself the course he will follow. The stories of past courage cannot supply courage itself. For this, each man must look into his own soul.'

"I pray that I can have the courage to make the right decision. Whatever is decided, whatever the future holds for me, I hope I shall be able to put this most recent tragedy behind me and make some future contribution to our state and mankind, whether it be in public or private life. Thank you and good night."

What did the media have to say about the Senator's address?

New York Times: "A carefully worked out plan to reestab-lish his political position in the eyes of the voters based upon a partially irrelevant and totally unsatisfactory ex parte account. There are so many gaping holes in the story which he has so assiduously avoided filling, there is such an unmistakable atmo-sphere of calculated evaluation for maximum—or, as the case may be, minimum—public effort that we cannot consider the matter to be satisfactorily resolved in any sense."

Washington Post: "Because it is crucial for the Senator to dispel the impression given by his silence that there is something he is trying to hide." His silence was "compelling evidence in support of the ugly suggestion that there was, and still is a care-ful, cold-blooded conspiracy to cover something up—a suspi-cion that, as things stand, is easily arrived at."

Dr. Edward Self, who had driven Chief Arena on Saturday morning, said that Kennedy's speech contained "discrepancies and hiatuses." If Kennedy had made a wrong turn onto Dike Road, Self said, "his headlights would have revealed water and the bridge in adequate time for him to stop the car. For him to drive off the bridge implied that judgment and reaction time were impaired."

These facts raised serious doubts of the accident description with Dr. Self, who is quoted as saying, "the highly polished, indeed, politically masterful TV statement of July 25 without retorting, 'Just who do you think you're kidding?'"

John Farrar said the speech didn't answer any questions, but invited more. He said if Kennedy was in shock, why didn't Gargan and Markham immediately contact police, if they were concerned enough to dive in to try to save Kopechne? He stated that if the fire department had been contacted, "there was a great possibility that we could have saved Mary Jo's life."

CHAPTER 4

MARY JO—EFFECTED THE MOST, CONSIDERED THE LEAST

Mary Jo Kopechne—pronounced Ko Pech Nee, rather than Ko Peck Nee, as most people and the media used—was born in Wilkes-Barre, Pennsylvania, on July 26, 1940, but spent most of her growing up years in East Orange, New Jersey. She missed her twenty-ninth birthday by just eight days.

Her parents, Joseph and Gwen, moved to New Jersey after World War II. He was an insurance salesman. Although both parents were very close to Mary Jo, their only child, Joe had a very special relationship with his beloved daughter.

Mary Jo, also called Jo by friends and family, was a very friendly, disciplined and religious girl. She earned a degree in education from the Caldwell Business College, and after graduation in 1962 went to work teaching for a semester or two at Catholic High in the Mobile-Birmingham diocese of Alabama under Father Paul Mullaney.

A friend who was working for the government in Washington, D.C. persuaded her to come live with her, and got Mary Jo a job as administrative assistant for Senator George Smathers. Mary Jo had always loved politics, and was a volunteer worker during JFK's campaign. Senator Smathers, from Florida, served for eighteen years, from 1951 to 1969. As much as she respected Senator Smathers, and enjoyed working for him, Mary Jo's great dream was to work for Senator Robert F. (Bobby) Kennedy.

She finally got the job she wanted with Senator Kennedy. She began working during the investigation into the Bobby Baker scandal. Then, Mary Jo became responsible for a specific geographic territory. It was her job to keep in contact with people in that territory, making certain that they were kept up-to-date on all issues the Senator supported. She also had responsibility for campaign funding and, of course, for ensuring election support.

Kennedy, the junior Senator from New York, was campaigning for the presidential nomination in 1968. Bobby selected Mary Jo, a dedicated and endless worker, as part of the group going to the Ambassador Hotel in Los Angeles to assist the Senator on the campaign trail. He was fatally wounded on June 5 in the hotel ballroom by Sirhan Sirhan, and died some twenty-five-and-a-half hours later at Good Samaritan Hospital.

Mary Jo returned on the train that brought Senator Kennedy's body back. After the funeral, she was given the responsibility of closing the office. She returned documents to the proper people, or filed them with the appropriate offices or departments. Any campaign funds had to be refunded to the donors, and other financial records filed with responsible authorities.

It was a difficult and thankless job, but Mary Jo performed it with her usual dedication and professionalism. She constantly thought about Bobby and the family. She was still devastated by the assassination, and by the loss of her "friend" and boss.

One family member brought up the following theory: What if Mary Jo found certain private papers that she felt should not be distributed or shared with others? Who would she turn to? The only remaining family member in an elective position was Ted. Was he someone she could trust?

During the time Mary Jo worked for the Senator, she became very close to the entire family, as well as their relatives and friends. She was not a stranger at Hyannis Port, spending countless weekends at the house and at the pool. Ethel Kennedy and the children were especially fond of her. After Bobby's death, Ethel offered Mary Jo a job as governess of the children. She declined, but still remained close to them.

Though time heals, Mary Jo constantly grieved for Bobby and his family. She went to work for a judge in D.C. She was excited when she was invited to the Regatta with her friends from the "Boiler Room." Though Bobby's office for the girls was called the "Boiler Room, it was, in fact, very spacious and sumptuous. The girls became known as the "Boiler Room" girls.

After the accident, there were some reports indicating that Mary Jo had a large number of drinks before the accident. Also, there were reports that she was pregnant.

A family spokesperson was very surprised upon hearing these reports. Regarding the drinking and allegedly high blood-alcohol level, the spokesperson said it was hard to believe; Mary Jo seldom had more than one drink, two at the most. When someone suggested that Mary Jo might have been forced to have more drinks, the response was "Mary Jo never did anything she didn't want to do."

There was also the suggestion that she was pregnant at the time. However, this spokesperson said that Mary Jo began her period a day or two before she left for the trip to Martha's Vineyard, and that she was close to being engaged to a foreign diplomat.

Aside from Mary Jo's death that fateful night, one family spokesperson related some happenings that were kept completely secret. According to this spokesperson, there were many more Kennedy family members and friends attending the Regatta than reported that weekend.

Reportedly, on the night of the accident, one of the Kennedy family members was brutally beat up by unknown assailants. No reason for this alleged attack was ever provided, because there was never any report of this supposed incident.

All of these unidentified Kennedys were immediately and secretly rushed off the island, according to this spokesperson.

Does this supposed incident have anything to do with Mary Jo's death? That's another unanswered question from the night of July 18, 1969.

After Mary Jo's death, the Kopechnes were deluged with hundreds and hundreds of letters from all over the world. Letters came from people who knew Mary Jo. But, surprisingly, many total strangers had an overwhelming need to reach out and comfort Gwen and Joe.

It was as if Mary Jo belonged to the world, and everyone shared in her loss. She was immediately taken into the hearts of the general public, and she has remained there after all these years.

In 1966, in recognition of her outstanding ability, accomplishments and service to her community, country and profession, she was selected as one of the Outstanding Young Women of America.

As one family spokesperson related, "All those who knew Mary Jo, praised her. And those who felt empathy for Gwen and Joe sought to comfort them. Then there were those who wanted to shake them until their teeth rattled for not being more vindictive, more aggressive towards Kennedy, more demanding for answers, an autopsy, money, and/or whatever."

Most of the letters received by the Kopechnes clearly described the type of person Mary Jo was.

"My only recollections of her are her cheerful, joyful disposition and her love of everything she did. Mary Jo was a good, wholesome girl—noone [sic] who knew her would ever doubt that. This is certainly an example of the saying, 'Our loss is heaven's gain.'"—Pat D. (date unknown)

"We really didn't become friends until we, quite by chance, happened to be teaching at Montgomery Catholic High. May you be assured that Mary Jo will remain in my thoughts and prayers."—Judy L. (7/23/69)

"My own feelings about the loss of Mary Jo run deep. I don't know of anyone who had quite the impact that M.J. had on me. Although a number of years younger, her spirit and zest set an example which I both admired and strived to emulate. I don't believe I've ever met anyone of such verve, wit and enthusiasm.

"And I've never met anyone who so admired her parents as did Mary Jo. I guess you knew that. It was always beautiful to hear Mary Jo talk of you—to see her pride and her love.

"I will always be grateful that I knew Mary Jo—though it was less than a year—because I'm richer for those months."—Cathy R. (2/2/70)

"I knew Mary Jo—not as well as I would have liked to—but enough to know what a truly fine person she was. She reflected her upbringing so thoroughly. She was kind and sweet and I don't remember anyone saying an unkind word about her in the few years I worked with her.

"Mary Jo was always there. In the time of crisis and urgent need, she was the one you could depend on. I remember many times on a weekend when a crisis would inevitably arise, hands and heads were needed and Mary Jo was always available. She'd give up an evening with her friends to do what was expected of her and never complained.

"That's why Bob Kennedy was so fond of her—but beyond that, he enjoyed her delightful sense of humor. Being a New Jerseyan myself, I was very proud of her when, in spite of the sophisticated voices around her, she would come out with a funny phrase that would have Bob laughing.

"What I'm trying to say, I know, will not assuage your terrible grief but I hope it will make you understand that we who worked with her and loved her for her gentle way, will miss her too, very much."—Angie N. (8/31/69)

"My memories of Mary Jo are all good ones; in the CYO plays, the campaign for JFK, and the few dates that we had. Her thoughtfulness was unbelievable. She truly was a credit to you, her school and the church.

"My wife and I can only pray that our little girls—Mary Kay (3) and Maureen (1)—will approach Mary Jo's excellence in character, devotion and perseverance."—Dick T. (10/10/69)

"Mary Jo did many things for me. When I left for Belgium two years ago she gave me a going away party; and a dinner party when Bobby and I were married. Mary Jo was the kind of person you knew would always be there in a pinch—she was a good reliable friend of ours and I miss her. I had spoken to her only a week before her death and she was planning on coming over—I say these things to you now, not to make you sadder, but rather, to let you know how fondly we feel towards Mary Jo."—Elly (8/14/69)

"I am the eighth Boiler Room girl. I am heartbroken over your tragic loss because Mary Jo was such a good friend to me. I wish there were something I could say that would be of comfort but I know there is little any of us can do or say. I pray for you and for the rest of us who must carry on without the added zest of Mary Jo's love of life and warmth. She was very kind and giving to her friends and there was no one who didn't like her. She brought each of us a little extra sparkle and I feel we are better for having known her.

"She was especially kind to me in my early days in the Senate office. because I think she sensed how lonely I was at the time. I've never forgotten that and always treasured our friendship. We shared the agonizing hours after the Senator was shot and the first hours after his death. I couldn't have made it though that difficult time without her."—Kay R. (7/23/69)

"Your daughter will long be remembered by many. She had a rare warmth of personality and beauty of character that left a lasting impression on all who met her."—Warren K. (7/27/69)

"Betsy and I were deeply shocked to learn about Mary Jo. I remember Mary Jo well, first as Betsy's roommate at Olive Avenue until Betsy and I were married and then from my visits to the girls in Georgetown whenever I was in Washington. I especially remember Mary Jo's cheerful enthusiasm. She frequently sent me newspaper clippings about my mountaineering friends and Betsy laughingly used to say that Mary Jo was my biggest fan."—Nick C. (7/23/69)

In order to perpetuate the memory of Mary Jo, a scholarship fund at Caldwell College for Women was established by a group of Boston area businessmen who were "impressed by the idealism manifested by Mary Jo."—Katherine C. (8/23/69)

CHAPTER 5

THE KOPECHNES—
JOE AND GWEN'S
NEVER-ENDING NIGHTMARE

The Kopechnes were a very close and loving family. Joe was nineteen and Gwen fifteen when they met. As soon as he saw Gwen, Joe says he knew he was going to marry her.

They were very devoted, and from the time Mary Jo was born, the family was very close. Their very warm relationship with Mary Jo was the most important aspect of their life.

Early in the morning of July 19, 1969, the Kopechnes received a phone call from Ted Kennedy telling them that their daughter had drowned the night before in an accident. Obviously, they were both in a state of shock. They were overwhelmed. What do you do at a time like this? All they could do was grieve. They couldn't believe what they had just heard. Their daughter was dead!

Within an hour or so, Dun Gifford arrived at the door. He introduced himself as a close confidante of the Kennedy family, and said that he was there to help them during this tragic time. He expressed his deepest sorrow.

Actually, he was sent there to take charge of all communications with friends, neighbors, the media and anyone else who wanted to contact the Kopechnes.

He immediately began to field phone calls. He wouldn't allow Gwen or Joe to talk to anyone. If a neighbor showed up at the door, he politely asked them to leave.

He shielded the Kopechnes from every contact. Monitored every call. He made sure the Kennedy team knew everything that was going on. He manipulated all the information supplied to Gwen and Joe relating to the accident. They didn't even know, at the time, the exact details of what had happened, or that Kennedy was even involved.

Joe made funeral arrangement at the Kielty Funeral Home. When Mary Jo's body arrived, it was taken directly there. Joe and Gwen believed their daughter had drowned in a swimming accident. They assumed an autopsy was held before the body was shipped.

After preparing Mary Jo for the burial, Mr. Kielty told the Kopechnes that there were no marks on her body. The woman who dressed Mary Jo's hair confirmed Mr. Kielty's assessment.

When District Attorney Dinis requested an autopsy months later, the Kopechnes were still grieving and in mourning. They did not want to exhume the body. A cardinal from Massachusetts supposedly encouraged Gwen and Joe not to have the autopsy. We say "supposedly" because years later, Gwen did not recall the incident which she had related earlier. They still didn't know all the details of the accident. They thought Mary Jo had died immediately. The Kennedy team had covered all bases and kept facts hidden from Mary Jo's parents.

The Kopechnes wanted more information. They wanted to talk with Senator Kennedy. The only time they had seen him was at the funeral. They continually tried to make contact with the Senator, but were unsuccessful. They talked with members of the Kennedy team, who were constantly around Gwen and Joe, monitoring their every movement. Finally, they heard from him. He told them to just go along with him, said there was more to this than meets the eye, and suggested the Kopechnes come up to Hyannis Port, and have a sit-down chat with the Senator to learn everything.

Gwen and Joe finally scheduled a visit. They were invited to Hyannis Port where, lo and behold, they walked into a big cocktail party, nothing like what they had been led to believe would happen, or what they expected. They looked around, but didn't recognize anyone. They were lost. Finally, Senator Kennedy appeared. After exchanging greetings with a number of guests, he came up to Gwen and Joe, shook hands, said hello, and walked away . . . never to be seen or heard from again.

The Kopechnes tried talking to the "Boiler Room" girls who attended the party on the Island that weekend. Each of the girls refused to talk, referring the Kopechnes to their respective lawyers.

After Mary Jo's death, the Kopechnes wanted to leave their home in New Jersey. It brought back too many memories of Mary Jo. They moved to the Poconos.

It took years, but finally the Kopechnes decided to visit Chappaquiddick. They wanted to view all the areas that Mary Jo had visited that fateful weekend—Katama Shores, the Lawrence Cottage, the Dike Bridge. They hoped to talk with people who were involved, people who knew Mary Jo.

During their trip, they met and talked with John Farrar. John told them he didn't believe that she had died immediately. He said that she didn't drown, that she could have been saved. If his department had been contacted immediately, there was no question in his mind that she would be alive today.

Joe lost control of his emotions when he heard this version of what happened. He couldn't believe that Mary Jo could still be alive. His only daughter did not have to die. After that day, Joe was never the same. He grieved himself right into cancer. He had operations, and coughed up blood. "Our girl," as Joe called his daughter, would never be with them again. She didn't have to die. He said, "They are very bad people." They never told us the truth and they wouldn't let us talk with anyone who could provide accurate information. They manipulated us.

Gwen Kopechne said the Kennedys stifled us. We never received an accurate account of what happened to our daughter. And, that's something that will live with us the rest of our lives. The "biggest mistake we ever made was not allowing the autopsy."

Joseph Kopechne born April 25, 1913, in Swoyersville, Pennsylvania, and died December 24, 2003.

Gwen Kopechne born June 8, 1918, in Kingston, Pennsylvania, and died December 20, 2007.

Chapter 6

Les Leland Background Information

Leslie Leland was born into a pharmaceutical family. His grandmother and grandfather had owned a drug store. His uncle ran a drug store. He was the second oldest of 6 children: four brothers (Chuck, Stevie, Jack, and Scott) and one sister, Judith. Born and raised in East Bridgewater, Massachusetts, a town of about 6,000 people just 30 miles south of Boston, Leslie always had one desire: he wanted to be a pharmacist and own his own drug store. He graduated from the Massachusetts College of Pharmacy in 1963. After graduation, he moved with his wife and first son to the Vineyard. He worked for several years in the drug store, which was then run by his late uncle. He bought his grandmother's pharmacy and took over management of Leslie's Drug Store in 1968.

In May, 1969, Leslie Leland was summoned for possible duty on a grand jury. The selected jurors' names were pulled out of a drum. The names already pulled were Mrs. Dionis C. Riggs, George T. Silva, Marie B. Nickerson, Theresa M. Morse, Lloyd Mayhew, Mrs. Helen M. Mosher, Frank G. Gibson, Sr., Russell Gentry, Merideth Gelinas, William Figueiredo, Richard H. Fitzpatrick, Arthur G. Doane, Mrs. Marie Crawley, Mrs. Dorothy M. Crowell, Ernest Correllus, Mrs. Yvette E. Canha,

Marvin M. Burnham, Mrs. Jean M. Bryant, Dwight P. Brown, Virginia Blakesley, and Mrs. Hilda Backus, leaving one more name to pull.

Les thought he was certainly out, which was fine with him. He had just bought the pharmacy and was trying to build his business. But the twenty-second and final name was pulled from the drum … Leslie H. Leland.

The first order of business for the grand jury was the selection of a foreman, with voting done by secret ballot. Les was selected as foreman, and he recalls thinking that this was the first time he'd ever won an election of any type.

The grand jury is impaneled for a year, and sits twice during that period. One of the first cases was an altercation in a bar, where a pharmacist's son drowned in his own blood. Les knew the pharmacist, making it a very tough first case for the foreman and the jury.

Leland first learned about the Chappaquiddick accident on Sunday evening.

"I was having dinner out with my wife. One of my fellow jurors came up and told us about the incident. Almost immediately, he asked what I was going to do about this matter. My first response was, 'I don't know, but I will find out what our responsibilities are.'

"On Monday morning after the Chappaquiddick tragedy, I opened the pharmacy and 'all hell broke loose.' The phones were ringing off the hook. 'What are you going to do about this?' was asked time and time again. In the store, the press was after me all the time. People in the store wanted answers. I was being bombarded.

"Here I am, 29 years old. Trying to run a business. I don't know what my responsibilities are. I don't know the answers. I'm not a lawyer. The D.A. is the expert. That's what he's paid to do. I don't know the law like he does.

"It wasn't only me. Everyone was being bombarded. The D.A. The Chief of Police. Everyone."

CHAPTER 7

A CLANDESTINE MEETING

A few days after the incident, Les was invited to a "clandestine meeting" with two key Vineyard officials.

"I received a call at Leslie's Drug store from the Chief of Police, Dominic J. (Jim) Arena. He said, 'Leslie, I think we need to meet to discuss the accident at Chappaquiddick.' I told him fine, come on over here to the drug store and we can talk. He said that wouldn't work because there are too many cameras and the news media is all over the place. I said, OK, I'll drive over to the Edgartown Police Station and we can talk there. Once again Arena said no. We can't do it there because the press is swarming all over the place. So I said, fine. You tell me where and when. That's when he suggested the Blinker Light."

Blinker Light, the only traffic light on the island, is located at the intersection of Barnes Road and Vineyard Haven/Edgartown Road, near the middle of the island.

They decided to meet that afternoon. Les drove to the selected location and saw a regular car parked there. An unmarked car, definitely not a police car: Nothing on the side of the car, no blue lights or extra antennas.

"I drove up and got out of my car, and a gentleman on the passenger side got out and opened the back door, motioning for me to get in. At that point I thought, well, this is very strange.

Who is this man? Certainly not Chief Arena. I was feeling very intimidated and fearful. What is going on?

"Once in the car, I recognized Chief Arena behind the steering wheel. Jim introduced the other man as Walter Steele, the county prosecutor. The Chief started the car, and we drove up Barnes Road to the Edgartown West Tisbury Road and continued on. The situation, as I said, was strange. They never even acknowledged my presence. All they did was carry on a conversation. I was intent on listening. To the best of my recollection it went something like:

"You know Walter, that was a terrible accident. It's got to be so hard on the Senator. He did everything he could to save that poor girl. He kept diving in, trying time after time, but the tides just made it too difficult for him and he finally became exhausted. He's lucky he's still alive.

Walter Steele replied, basically saying: "I know, Chief. It's that Kennedy curse again. Seems like nothing can go right for that family. The oldest son is killed in the war. Jack is killed in Dallas. Then it's Bobby who gets shot and killed. And here's the Senator, the last one left. I really feel sorry for him. Here he is. A Senator. Hoping to follow his brother's footsteps into the presidency. And then this happens."

The Chief kept saying something like: "We investigated every single issue, and checked every piece of evidence, and there is no way it was anything but a terrible accident. As you know, the coroner said it was a drowning. We got Kennedy's statement about that evening. About the only thing you might say he could be guilty of is a minor traffic violation."

"Walter Steele was quick to point out that Jim and the others who investigated the accident covered every aspect of what could have happened, and everyone came to the same conclusion. So, I really don't see any need of any further action. There's no reason for further investigation or a trial or anything."

"Chief Arena responded that, yeah, if we could only get rid of the press, but they're determined to create something just to keep people reading their newspapers, or listening to their reports. If it wasn't for them, this whole thing could be forgotten."

Les Leland said, "I didn't really comment one way or the other; I just listened.

"Finally, we got back to the Blinker Light. I got out, said goodbye, and drove back home. I was still scratching my head, trying to figure out the reason for this bizarre encounter. It shook me up. Intimidated me. Why had they invited me along for the ride? Why they didn't even acknowledge me, or ask me anything? It became obvious that as foreman of the grand jury, they wanted to impress upon me that there was no reason for any further investigation. Absolutely no reason whatsoever for the grand jury to get involved. This was simply a terrible accident. Unfortunately, a young lady drowned."

Senator Kennedy's car being removed from Poucha Pond

CHAPTER 8

THE D.A.

Edmund S. Dinis was the District Attorney of the Southern District of Massachusetts at the time of the accident. Simultaneously, he was up for re-election on the Democratic ticket. Les looked to Dinis for assistance in what to do and how to do it.

After the Chappaquiddick incident, Les had many discussions with Dinis. He kept asking about his responsibilities and obligations as foreman, but never could get any clear and concise answers. It was extremely frustrating to Leland. Early on, Dinis kept telling Les that it was just an accident. The media kept asking Leland what he was going to do about an investigation and/or grand jury action. They told him that he had the right to call for an investigation. He was still unclear about his responsibilities and duties. That's why he kept talking to the D.A., in hope of finding out.

At least some of the media indicated that Les was intent on investigating the accident. But for the first few weeks and months, Leland was simply asking questions concerning the correct and proper grand jury procedures. As Les stated, "You have to remember, a grand jury is made up of lay people; they are not lawyers and they are not skilled in the legal profession. A grand jury takes its direction from the district attorney.

"As I look back on my relationship with Dinis, I now understand his approach, which I didn't at the time. His response to my efforts was: 'Well, you have the right to investigate this accident.' My response was 'Why don't you investigate, you're the district attorney—you are the one who is skilled and you're paid to do that job, that's your profession.'"

But Dinis ignored Leland's efforts and requests for the D.A. to take action, and kept prompting Les to do the investigation.

Leland contacted the state attorney general, asking the same questions. The state attorney general gave a different answer. Leland was told that the district attorney was the one who should investigate.

Les knew, though, that Dinis didn't want to get involved and was clearly passing the buck back to him.

"I didn't understand why at the time, but I certainly do now. Dinis was a Democrat, up for re-election, and probably had some ties with the Kennedys. He was in a situation where if the grand jury instigated the call for an investigation, he could then say to his fellow Democrats, 'Look, I'm doing a job that I have to because I am the district attorney. The grand jury called for the investigation, not me.' Whereas, if he had initiated it, it wouldn't sit so well with the political machinery."

Les continued, "So, I went through that ordeal. I had the same conversation with Dinis several times, because he was still pushing for me to do it. Eventually, Dinis did get involved. He went to Pennsylvania to try to exhume Mary Jo's body in order to perform an autopsy. After that effort failed, Dinis considered calling for an inquest. At that point in time, the media pretty much left me alone because of Dinis' involvement.

"The grand jury met in the fall of 1969 for regularly scheduled business. Of course, all of the jurors wanted to know what was happening to the Kennedy situation. I told them what I had done and the little I knew. Dinis explained to all of us why he was now going to pursue an inquest, which was a fact-finding mission.

"He promised the jurors he would keep me informed of the proceedings and investigation. All of the jurors felt comfortable with that approach. During his statement and explanation, Dinis told us that he didn't want to bring the grand jury into the picture, but again assured all of us that he would be in constant contact with me, as the foreman.

"Shortly thereafter, the district attorney officially announced that he was going to call for an inquest to look into this 'accident'."

Later, Dinis stated: "There's no question in my mind that the grand jury would have brought an indictment against Ted Kennedy for manslaughter, if I had given them the case." It is also interesting that Dinis previously had directed police chiefs in his district to charge "all defendants accused of operating under the influence of liquor when such operation resulted in the death of another person with manslaughter."

All complaints were to be sent to the Superior Court if probable cause was found, and only a judge could dismiss any complaint, not a prosecutor or police officer.

It's automatic in Massachusetts for the prosecutor to bring action for criminal manslaughter when a person is killed in an accident. There must be a hearing. The rule is clear: "Any person who wantonly or in a reckless or grossly negligent manner did that which resulted in the death of a human being was guilty of manslaughter, although he did not contemplate such a result."

Consider also that John Farrar, a scuba diver with the fire department who removed the body from the submerged vehicle, stated that he believed that Mary Jo Kopechne might have lived for some time under-water by breathing a bubble of trapped air, and could have been saved if rescue assistance had been summoned immediately.

Calling for an inquest was not the proper course of action. Inquests, today, are an antiquated procedure, a rarely used investigative measure. The rules were not being followed. What should have happened didn't happen. Then, to top everything off, the powers-that-be made the inquest secretive, so that attendance was limited only to those testifying. When the inquest ended, the transcript was immediately impounded, and was not publicly available. The Kennedy legal team demanded this secrecy, even though inquests are supposed to be open to the public.

No one knew what had happened, and the only legal block in the way was the grand jury. Leland and Dinis had several discussions, with Leland learning a few of the things that went on at the inquest. Dinis told Leland it would be really interesting if the grand jury went back into session to look at the inquest, because there were a lot of gray areas.

In the days and weeks after the incident, Leland kept communicating with Dinis. He kept insisting that it was necessary for the district attorney to investigate the accident, and that it was within Dinis' job description. He supposedly was the expert. But nothing happened.

Leland called a meeting with Dinis and Attorney General Robert Quinn. He wanted to know what the rights of the grand jury were. What action could the grand jury take? What could and couldn't they do? Leland wanted to know because the press was pressuring him to investigate, to get the grand jury involved. Attorney General Quinn told Leland that the grand jury had no legal right to call for an investigation at that time. The decision was up to the attorney general, district attorney or a judge.

This opinion was completely opposite than that of Dinis. Leland said, "Talk about confusion. Who do you believe?"

From all the conversations, Leland surmised Dinis did not want any part of the case or a grand jury investigation. What he didn't know was that Quinn had given him the incorrect information; the grand jury had every right to investigate the matter.

In September 1969, Leland wrote to the Chief Justice of the Superior Court asking that the grand jury be allowed back in session to investigate the incident at Chappaquiddick. He was told this would not be possible before an inquest was called into session.

CHAPTER 9

KENNEDY TESTIMONY

Dinis did call for an inquest, which began January 5, 1970. The problem was that for all practical purposes inquests were obsolete. The inquest was only a fact-finding procedure. Based on the testimony given at the inquest, only the judge or district attorney could recommend that the case be turned over to the grand jury.

Originally, the inquest was supposed to be open to the press and the public. But Kennedy's attorneys appealed to the Massachusetts Supreme Court. The inquest judge, James A. Boyle, ruled that these sessions were to be open because the public was entitled to know. Kennedy's lawyers won the appeal. An eighty-two-year-old inquest rule was overturned for Kennedy. The inquest proceedings were closed to the public and the media. Ultimately, Kennedy's lawyers convinced Judge Boyle to impound the transcripts of the inquest until all legal actions had been exhausted. That left Kennedy with only Leland to contend with in the foreman's search for the truth.

Senator Kennedy was the first witness called. Here is the testimony he gave at the inquest. Or should we say, perhaps, the doctored testimony? After he testified, his lawyers reportedly went to a house about 100 yards from the courthouse. The Senator's testimony, as determined by staff notes and memory, was dictated to a court stenographer hired by Kennedy lawyers. So, in effect, they had a script of what the Senator had actually said in the courtroom under oath at the inquest.

THE COURT: Senator, would you take the witness stand?

KENNEDY: Yes.

Examination by Mr. Dinis:

Q: Please give your name to the court.

A: Edward Moore Kennedy.

Q: And where is your legal residence, Mr. Kennedy?

A: Three Charles River Square, Boston.

Q: Directing your attention to July 18, 1969, were there plans made by you to have a gathering on Martha's Vineyard Island?

A: There were.

Q: And what were these plans, Mr. Kennedy?

A: There were plans to participate in an annual sailing regatta in Edgartown on the dates of Friday, July eighteenth, and Saturday, July nineteenth, and with my cousin Joe Gargan, Mr. Markham, Mr. LaRosa and a number of other people, a number of other individuals.

Q: When were these plans made?

A: Well, I had planned to participate in the regatta for some period of weeks.

Q: And were there any particular arrangements made for this gathering that we have just discussed?

A: Well, I had entered my boat in the regatta and had listed my crew. I had made those arrangements through my cousin, Joe Gargan.

Q: Were there any arrangements made to rent a house on Chappaquiddick?

A: I had made no such arrangements myself.

Q: Do you know who did?

A: Yes, I do.

Q: May we have that name?

A: Mr. Gargan.

Q: Mr. Gargan. When did you arrive on the Island in conjunction with this gathering?

A: On July eighteenth, about one o'clock.

Q: One p.m.?

A: That is correct.

Q: Was there anyone with you?

A: No, I arrived by myself.

Q: And where did you stay, Senator?

A: Well, at the Shiretown Inn.

Q: Could you tell the court what your activities were during the afternoon from the time of your arrival?

A: Well, I arrived shortly after one o'clock on July eighteenth, was met by Mr. John B. Crimmins, driven through town, made a brief stop to pick up some fried clams, traveled by ferry to Chappaquiddick Island to a small cottage and changed into another bathing suit; later visited the beach on, I imagine, the east side of that island for a brief swim, returned to the cottage and changed into another bathing suit, returned to the ferry slip and waded out to my boat, the *Victura*, and later participated in a race which ended at approximately six o'clock.

Q: When did you check into the Shiretown Inn that day?

A: Sometime after 6:30, before seven o'clock.

Q: Was anyone else in your party staying at the Shiretown Inn?

A: My cousin, Joe Gargan.

Q: Did your nephew, Joseph Kennedy, stay there?

A: Not to my knowledge.

Q: Now, following your checking in at the Shiretown Inn, what were your activities after that?

A: I returned to my room, visited with a few friends just prior to returning to that room on the porch, which is outside the room of the Shiretown–outside my room at the Shiretown Inn–washed up briefly and returned to Chappaquiddick Island.

Q: What time did you return to Chappaquiddick Island at that time?

A: It was sometime shortly after seven o'clock.

Q: And these friends that you had some conversation with at the Shiretown, do you have their names?

A: I do.

Q: May we have them?

A: Well, they are Mr. Ross Richards, I believe Mr. Stanley Moore was there that evening, and perhaps one or two of their crew, maybe Mrs. Richards. I am not familiar with the names. I know the other members of his crew, but I would say a group of approximately five or six.

Q: Do you recall the number of the room in which you were staying?

A: I believe it was nine. Seven or nine.

Q: Now, you say you returned to Chappaquiddick around 7:30 p.m.?

A: About 7:30.

Q: About that time. Now, were you familiar with the island of Chappaquiddick? Had you been there before?

A: Never been on Chappaquiddick Island before that day.

Q: I believe you did state in one of your prepared statements that you had been visiting this island for about 30 years?

A: Martha's Vineyard Island.

Q: But you had never been to Chappaquiddick?

A: Never been to Chappaquiddick before 1:30 on the day of July eighteenth.

Q: Now, when you left the Shiretown Inn and returned to Chappaquiddick around 7:30 p.m., was there anyone with you?

A: Mr. Crimmins.

THE COURT: Might I just impose a moment and ask this question? You said you took a swim on Chappaquiddick Island Friday afternoon?

KENNEDY: That is correct.

THE COURT: Did you travel over the Dike Bridge to go to the beach on that swim?

KENNEDY: Yes, I did. If Your Honor would permit me, at the time of the afternoon upon arrival on Chappaquiddick Island, as at the time I was met at Martha's Vineyard Airport, I was driven by Mr. Crimmins to the cottage and to the beach, [and] returned to the cottage subsequent to the point of rendezvous with the Victoria.

Q: What automobile was being used at that time?

A: A four-door Oldsmobile '88.

THE COURT: Might I ask you just a question? Who drove you to the beach?

KENNEDY: Mr. Crimmins.

THE COURT: Was the car operated over the Dike Bridge, or was it left on the side?

KENNEDY: No, it was operated over the Dike Bridge.

Q: Was there anyone at the cottage when you arrived there at 7:30 p.m.?

A: No, I don't believe so.

Q: Had there been anyone there when you changed your swimming suits early in the afternoon?

A: Not when I first arrived there. Subsequently, a group returned to the cottage after the swim.

Q: When you returned?

A: They were either outside the cottage or in its immediate vicinity. I wasn't aware whether they were inside the cottage or outside, at the time I changed.

Q: Do you have the names of these persons who were there?

A: I can only give them in a general way, because I am not absolutely sure which people were there at that particular time, and which were in town making arrangements.

Q: Were part of the group there later that evening?

A: Yes, they were.

Q: Were there any persons other than the crew that participated in the cookout there?

A: No.

Q: Were there any other automobiles at that house on Chappaquiddick that afternoon?

A: Yes, there were.

Q: Do you know how many?

A: Just two, to my best knowledge. One other vehicle, so there were two in total to my best knowledge.

Q: Did you have any plans at that time to stay on Chappaquiddick Island?

A: No, I did not.

Q: Did you plan on staying overnight?

A: No, I did not.

Q: And how long did you actually stay on Chappaquiddick Island that evening?

A: Well, to my best knowledge, I would say 1:30 in the morning on July nineteenth.

THE COURT: When you left?

KENNEDY: When I left.

Q. What transpired after you arrived at the cottage after your arrival at 7:30 p.m.?

A: Well, after my arrival, I took a bath in the tub that was available at the cottage, which was not available at the Shiretown Inn, and soaked my back; I later was joined by Mr. Markham, who arrived some time about eight o'clock, engaged in conversations with Mr. Markham until about 8:30, and the rest of the group arrived at 8:30 or shortly thereafter. During this period of time, Mr. Crimmins made me a drink of rum and Coca-Cola.

Q: Now, did you have dinner at the cottage?

A: Well, at 8:30 the rest of the group arrived and were made to feel relaxed and at home, enjoyed some hors d'oeuvres, were served a drink, those who wanted them, and steaks were cooked on an outdoor burner by Mr. Gargan at about approximately quarter of 10:00, I would think.

Q: Do you recall who did the cooking? Was there any cooking at that time?

A: Yes, there was.

Q: And do you recall who performed the job?

A: Well, principally Mr. Gargan. I think the young ladies did some of the cooking of the hors d'oeuvres and some of the gentlemen helped in starting the charcoal fire and also the cooking of the steaks, the making of the salad, and so forth.

Q: Were there any drinks served, cocktails served?

A: There were.

Q: Did anyone in particular tend bar or have charge of this particular responsibility?

A: Well, I tried initially to respond to any of the requests of the guests when they arrived, and then I think most of the individuals made their drinks after that that they wanted.

Q: And I believe you said earlier that Mr. Gargan was in charge of the arrangements of renting the cottage and making the preparation for the cookout, as far as you know?

A: That is correct. I would say the other gentlemen did some of the purchasing of the food, and others got the stuff for the cookout. Others—some brought the steaks, others brought the other ingredients for the cookout.

Q: Did you have occasion to leave the cottage at any time during that evening?

A: That is correct.

Q: Did you leave more than once?

A: That is correct.

Q: Well, will you please give us the sequence of events with regard to your activities after 8:30 p.m.?

A: Well, during the course of the evening, as I mentioned, I engaged in conversation and recollections with those that were attending this group, which were old friends of myself and our families. Some alcoholic beverages were served.

THE COURT: Excuse me. Read that question back to me.

[Question read]

Q: How many times did you leave the cottage that evening, Senator?

A: Two different occasions.

Q: Would you please tell us about the first time?

A: The first time I left was at approximately 11:15 the evening of July eighteenth, and I left a second time, sometime after midnight, by my best judgment it would be approximately 12:15 for the second time. On the second occasion, I never left the cottage itself; I left the immediate vicinity of the cottage, which was probably fifteen or twenty feet outside the front door.

Q: And when you left the second time, did you then return to Edgartown?

A: Sometime after I left the second time, I returned to Edgartown. I did not return immediately to Edgartown.

Q: Now, when you left on the first occasion, were you alone?

A: I was not alone.

Q: And who was with you?

A: Miss Mary Jo Kopechne was with me.

Q: Anyone else?

A: No.

Q: And did you use the '88 Oldsmobile that was later taken from the river?

A: I used—yes, I did.

Q: What time did Miss Kopechne arrive at the cottage that evening?

A: My best knowledge, approximately 8:30.

Q: At 8:30 p.m.?

A: That is correct.

Q: Do you know how she arrived?

A: To my best knowledge, she arrived in a White Valiant that brought some of the people to the party.

Q: Do you know who owned that car?

A: I believe it was a rented car.

Q: Do you know who rented it?

A: No. One of the group that was there, I would say. I'm not sure.

Q: When you left at 11:15 with Miss Kopechne, had you had any prior conversation with her?

A: Yes, I had.

Q: Will you please give that conversation to the court?

A: At 11:15 I was talking with Miss Kopechne, perhaps for some minutes before that period of time. I noticed the time, desired to leave and return to the Shiretown Inn, and indicated to her that I was leaving and returning to town. She indicated to me that she was desirous of leaving, if I would be kind enough to drop her back at her hotel. I said, well, I'm leaving immediately; spoke with Mr. Crimmins, requested the keys for the car and left at that time.

Q: Does Mr. Crimmins usually drive your car, or drive you?

A: On practically every occasion.

Q: On practically every occasion?

A: Yes.

Q: Was there anything in particular that changed those circumstances at this particular time?

A: Only to the extent that Mr. Crimmins, as well as some of the other fellows that were attending the cookout, were concluding their meal, enjoying the fellowship, and it didn't appear to me to be necessary to require him to bring me back to Edgartown.

Q: Do you know whether or not Miss Kopechne had her pocketbook with her at the time you left?

A: I do not.

Q: Mr. Kennedy, how were you dressed at the time you left the first time at 11:15?

A: In a pair of light slacks and a dark jersey, and I believe shoes, moccasins, and a back brace.

Q: Do you know how Miss Kopechne was dressed, do you recall that?

A: Only from what I have read in the—I understand, slacks and a blouse, sandals, perhaps a sweater; I'm not completely—

Q: And when you left the house at Chappaquiddick at 11:15, you were driving?

A: That is correct.

Q: And where was Miss Kopechne seated?

A: In the front seat.

Q: Was there any other person—was there any other person in that car at that time?

A: No.

Q: Was there any other item, thing, or object in the car at that time of any size?

A: Well, not to my knowledge at that particular time. I have read subsequently in newspapers that there was another person in that car, but that is only what I have read about and to my knowledge at that time there wasn't any other object that I was aware of.

Q: Well, Senator, was there any other person in the car?

A: No, there was not.

Q: And on leaving the cottage, Senator—Mr. Kennedy, where did you go?

A: Well, I traveled down, I believe it is Main Street, took a right on Dike Road and drove off the bridge at Dike Bridge.

Q: Did you at any time drive into Cemetery Road?

A: At no time did I drive into Cemetery Road.

(Note: Interesting that someone who claimed he had never been to the Island before would be so adamant about knowing he did not drive on Cemetery Road)

Q: Did you back up at any time?

A: At no time did I back that car up.

Q: Did you see anyone on the road between the cottage and the bridge that night?

A: I saw no one on the road between the cottage and the bridge.

THE COURT: Did you stop the car at any time?

KENNEDY: I did not stop the car at any time.

Q: (By Mr. Dinis) Did you pass any other vehicle at that time?

A: I passed no other vehicle at that time. I passed no other vehicle and I saw no other person and I did not stop the car at any time between the time I left the cottage and went off the bridge.

Q: Now, would you describe your automobile to the court?

A: Well, it is a four-door black sedan, Oldsmobile.

Q: Do you recall the registration plate?

A: I do not recall the registration plate.

Q: Senator, I show you a photograph and ask you whether of not you can identify that?

A: I believe that to be my car.

Q: Your automobile?

A: Yes.

MR DINIS: This is the automobile that the Senator identifies as his.

THE COURT: I think we ought to have a little more. This location is—

KENNEDY: I have no—

THE COURT: Mr. Kennedy says this is his automobile after the accident, and he doesn't know the location of where the automobile is or when this picture was taken. Mark that Exhibit 1.

Q: (By Mr. Dinis) I show you two photographs. Are you able to identify the automobile in the photographs?

A: In my best judgment, that is my automobile that went off the bridge.

Q: In examining the registration plate, would that help you at all?

A: I would believe that is my vehicle.

MR.DINIS: If Your Honor please, these are photographs that have been taken of the car which has been removed from the water.

THE COURT: Well, are you going to have any witness testify when these were taken?

MR.DINIS: Yes, Your Honor, we can have that.

THE COURT: And where they were taken?

MR. DINIS: Yes, Your Honor.

THE COURT: You identify the car as being your car?

KENNEDY: I do, Your Honor, it is my best judgment that is my car. I don't think there is really much question.

THE COURT: I would prefer that you wait until you put on the witness that is going to say—

MR. DINIS: May it be allowed de bene, Your Honor? The sequence in presenting this evidence for the purpose of—we couldn't—all I want to establish is that the Senator says they look like his car and then we will later have testimony as to where they were taken.

THE COURT: Well, I would rather not get into the trial technique.

MR. DINIS: I appreciate that.

THE COURT: De bene. I prefer you wait until you have the witness to identify it. I want to avoid as much as possible, Mr. Dinis, any trial technique.

KENNEDY: I would just say to the best knowledge that those are pictures of my car that were shown to me.

Q: (By Mr. Dinis) In your conversation with Miss Kopechne prior to your leaving at 11:15, did she indicate to you any necessity for returning to Martha's Vineyard or to Edgartown?

A: Prior to that conversation, no.

Q: Well, when she left with you, where was she going?

A: Back to her hotel.

Q: Now, when you left at 11:15, do you know how many persons remained at the house on Chappaquiddick?

A: To my best judgment, most of them were in the cottage when I left. I didn't make a count of who was there, but I think most of them were there.

THE COURT: Well, do you know of anyone having left before?

KENNEDY: No, I don't, except on one occasion where—

THE COURT: No, I mean having left permanently.

KENNEDY: No, no.

Q: (By Mr. Dinis) Did anyone else have access to your automobile that afternoon or that evening?

A: Oh, yes.

Q: And who might have that been?

A: Well, Mr. Crimmins certainly had access that afternoon, and I believe Mr. Tretter borrowed the car to return to Edgartown briefly. I couldn't say of my own knowledge that he used that car rather than the Valiant, but he may very well have, and I would say during the course of the afternoon it was generally available to any of the group to use for transportation.

Q: Do you recall how fast you were driving when you made the right on Dike Road?

A: No, I would say approximately seven or eight miles an hour.

(Note: Can you imagine driving down a paved road on the way to the ferry, at seven or eight miles per hour? Also, consider that reports indicated the car was going much, much faster than that on the dirt road.)

Q: And what were the lighting conditions and weather conditions that evening?

A: Well, as you know, there are no lights on that road. The road was dry. There was a reasonable amount of humidity. The night was clear, extremely dark.

Q: Were the windows opened or closed of the automobile?

A: Some of the windows were open and some were closed.

Q: Do you have an air conditioner in that car?

A: No, I don't.

THE COURT: Could we know which were opened and which were closed?

KENNEDY: I read, Your Honor—

THE COURT: No, not, of your own knowledge?

KENNEDY: Of my own knowledge?

THE COURT: What about the window on your side?

KENNEDY: I would expect it was open.

THE COURT: You don't remember that?

KENNEDY: I don't remember that.

THE COURT: How about the window on the passenger's side?

KENNEDY: I really don't remember.

THE COURT: Was it a warm night?

KENNEDY: I would think it was cool at that hour, but I really have no personal knowledge as to which windows were open or closed. I have read subsequently which ones were open or blown open, but at that time I really don't recall.

Q: (By Mr. Dinis) Well, Mr. Kennedy, was the window on the driver's side, the driver's door open?

A: Yes, it was.

(Note: a few moments earlier, when questioned by the judge, he said he didn't know.)

Q: Do you recall whether or not the window in the rear seat behind the driver was open?

A: I don't recall.

Q: And you have no recollection as to the windows on the passenger's side of the vehicle?

A: No, I really don't.

Q: How fast were you driving on Dike Road?

A: Approximately twenty miles an hour.

(Note: Let's see … he was driving down a paved road before he turned onto the dirt road at seven or eight miles an hour, but he's going twenty miles an hour down a dirt and gravel road?)

Q: Were the brakes of your Oldsmobile in order at that time?

A: I believe so. There is no reason to assume otherwise. Mr. Crimmins takes very good care of the car.

Q :Well, were you aware at the time that you were driving on a dirt road when you hit, when you turned onto Dike Road?

A: Well, sometime during the drive down Dike Road I was aware that I was on an unpaved road, yes.

Q: At what point, Mr. Kennedy, did you realize that you were driving on a dirt road?

A: Just sometime when I was—I don't remember any specific time when I knew I was driving on an unpaved road. I was generally aware sometime during the going down that road that it was unpaved, like many of the other roads here in Martha's Vineyard and Nantucket and Cape Cod.

(Note: do you think that if you were sober and driving down a paved road, and then turned onto a rough dirt-and-gravel road, you wouldn't know immediately?)

Q: When you left the house at 11:15, what was your destination?

A: The Katama Shores, the ferry slip, the Katama Shores, Shiretown.

Q: Now, had you been over that road from the ferry slip to the cottage more than once that day?

A: Yes, I had..

Q: Did you recall at the time that you noticed you were driving on a dirt road, that road from the ferry slip to the house had been paved?

A: Well, Mr. Dinis, I would say that I, having lived on Cape Cod and having visited these islands, I am aware some roads are paved.

THE COURT: I am sorry, that is not quite responsive. The question is whether or not you realized the road from the ferry to the cottage was paved.

MR. DINIS: That is correct.

KENNEDY: Yes.

THE COURT: That is, did you become aware of it during your two trips?

KENNEDY: Well, I would just say it was not of particular notice to me whether it was paved or unpaved

(Note: Do you think that if you drove several times on a bumpy, unpaved road, you would remember it?)

THE COURT: Were you driving the car in either one of those times?

KENNEDY: I was not.

Q: (By Mr. Dinis) Well, while you were driving down Dike Road, and after you noticed it was a dirt road and you were driving at twenty miles an hour, what happened, Mr. Kennedy?

A: Well, I became—

THE COURT: I'm going to ask one question. At any time after you got on the unpaved road, the so-called Dike Road, did you have the realization that you were on the wrong road?

KENNEDY: No.

(Note: Can you imagine what a jury might think of this testimony?)

THE COURT: Do you remember the question?

KENNEDY: After I realized it was an unpaved road, what did I become aware of?

Q: (By Mr. Dinis) Well, after you realized it was an unpaved road and that you were driving at twenty miles an hour, what happened then?

A: I went off Dike Bridge, or I went off a bridge.

Q: You went off a bridge into the water?

A: That is correct.

Q: Did you apply the brakes of that automobile prior to going off into the water?

A: Perhaps a fraction of a second before.

Q: What prompted you to do that?

A: Well, I was about to go off a bridge, and I applied the brakes.

Q: Were there any lights in that area?

A: Absolutely no lights in that area I noticed, other than the lights on my vehicle.

(Note: We know there were two lights on at that time.)

Q: Did you realize at that moment that you were not heading for the ferry?

A: At the moment I went off the bridge, I certainly did.

Q: Do you recall whether or not the—strike that question— well, what happened after that, Senator?

A: Well, I remembered the vehicle itself just beginning to go off the Dike Bridge, and the next thing I recall is the movement of Mary Jo next to me, the struggling, perhaps hitting or kicking me, and I, at this time, opened my eyes and realized I was upside down, that water was crashing in on me, that it was pitch black. I knew that and I was able to get a half a gulp, I would say, of air before I became completely immersed in the water. I realized that Mary Jo and I had to get out of the car. I can remember reaching down to try and get the doorknob of the car, and lifting the door handle and pressing against the door, and it not moving. I can remember reaching what I thought was down, which was really up, to where I thought the window was, and feeling along the side to see if the window was open, and the window was closed (Note: Didn't he say he thought the driver's side window was open?), and I can remember the last sensation of being completely out of air and inhaling what must have been a half a lung full of water, and assuming that I was going to drown, and the full realization that no one was going to be looking for us that night until the next morning, and that I wasn't going to get out of that car alive, and then somehow I can remember coming up to the last energy of just pushing, pressing, and coming up to the surface.

Q: Senator, how did you realize that you were upside down in the car?

A: Because—that was a feeling that I had as soon as I became aware that—the water rushing in and the blackness, I knew that I was, I felt I was upside down. I really wasn't sure of anything, but I thought I was upside down.

Q: Were you aware that the windows on the passenger's side were blown out of the car, were smashed?

A: I have read that subsequently. I wasn't aware of it at the time.

Q: Were you aware that there was any water rushing in on the passenger's side?

A: There was complete blackness. Water seemed to rush in from every point, from the windshield, from underneath me, above me. It almost seemed like you couldn't hold the water back even with your hands. What I was conscious of was the rushing of the water, the blackness, the fact that it was impossible to even hold it back.

Q: And you say, at that time, you had a thought to the effect that you may not be found until morning?

A: I was sure that I was going to drown.

Q: Did you make any observations of the condition of Miss Kopechne at that time?

A: At what time?

Q: At that particular moment when you were thrashing around in the car?

A: Well, at the moment I was thrashing around I was trying to find a way that we both could get out of the car, and at some time after I tried the door and the window I became convinced I was never going to get out.

Q: Was the window closed at that time?

A: The window was open.

Q: On the driver's side?

A: That's correct.

(Note: Whoops … didn't he just testify to something different?)

Q: And did you go through the window to get out of the car?

A: I have no idea in the world how I got out of that car.

Q: Do you have any recollection as to how the automobile left the bridge and went over into the water?

A: How it left the bridge?

Q: Yes. What particular path did it take?

A: No.

Q: Did it turn over?

A: I have no idea.

THE COURT: I would like to inquire, Mr. Dinis, something about the operation of the car, if you are finished.

MR. DINIS: Go right ahead, Your Honor.

THE COURT: You are driving along the dike sandy road and you are approaching the Dike Bridge. Now, can you describe to me what you saw, what you did, what happened from the point when first you saw the bridge?

KENNEDY: I would estimate that time to be fractions of a second from the time that I first saw the bridge and was on the bridge.

THE COURT: Did you have on your high beams, do you remember?

KENNEDY: I can't remember.

THE COURT: Is it your custom to use high beams when you are driving?

KENNEDY: I rarely drive. I really couldn't tell you. I may have.

THE COURT: It is recommended.

KENNEDY: It is recommended, but sometimes if there is a mist you see better with low beams.

THE COURT: Did you see the bridge before you actually reached it?

KENNEDY: The split second before I was on it.

THE COURT: Did you see that it was at an angle to the road?

KENNEDY: The bridge was at an angle to the road?

THE COURT: Yes.

KENNEDY: Just before going on it I saw that.

THE COURT: Did you make any attempt to turn your wheels to follow that angle?

KENNEDY: I believe I did, Your Honor. I would assume that I did try to go on the bridge. It appeared to me at that time that the road went straight.

THE COURT: Were you looking ahead at the time you were driving the car, at that time?

KENNEDY: Yes, I was.

THE COURT: Your attention was not diverted by anything else?

KENNEDY: No, it wasn't.

THE COURT: I don't want to foreclose you, Mr. Dinis. I want to look into the question of alcoholic beverages. Perhaps you had that in mind later?

MR. DINIS: Yes, Your Honor

THE COURT: All right.

Q: Going back to the cottage earlier in the day, you stated, you volunteered the information that you had a rum and Coca-Cola?

A: That is right.

Q: Did you have more than one?

A: Yes, I did.

Q: How many did you have?

A:I had two.

THE COURT: What time was this?

KENNEDY: The first was about eight o'clock.

THE COURT: I would like to go back before that, I think that you said you visited some friends at the Shiretown Inn?

KENNEDY: That is right.

THE COURT: Did you do some drinking then?

KENNEDY: I had about a third of beer at that time.

THE COURT: And you had nothing further until this?

KENNEDY: No, I had nothing further.

Q: And when did you have this second rum and Coke?

A: The second some time later on in the evening. I think before dinner, sometime about 9:15. It would be difficult for me to say.

Q: Now, during the afternoon of the eighteenth, did you have occasion to spend some time with your nephew, Joseph Kennedy?

A: I might have greeted him in a brief greeting, but otherwise, no. I know he was concerned about where he was going to stay, that he had some reservations and that somehow they had gotten cancelled, but I would say other than a casual passing and a greeting, I would say no.

Q: He was at this time on Chappaquiddick Island?

A: Not to my knowledge. I never saw him at Chappaquiddick.

Q: Did you see him at the Shiretown Inn?

A: I might have seen him in inquiring whether he could stay at the Shiretown Inn.

Q: Did he stay with you in your room?

A: No, he did not.

THE COURT: I would like to ask some questions. You said you had a portion of beer late in the afternoon at the Shiretown Inn?

KENNEDY: That is correct.

THE COURT: Then you had two rums and Coke at this cottage at Chappaquiddick Island some time after you arrived at about 8:30?

KENNEDY: That is right.

THE COURT: Who poured those drinks?

KENNEDY: Mr. Crimmins poured the first one. I poured the second one.

THE COURT: What amount of rum did you put in?

KENNEDY: It would be difficult, Your Honor, to estimate.

THE COURT: Well, by ounces.

KENNEDY: By ounces? I suppose two ounces.

THE COURT: I mean, some people pour heavy drinks. Some pour light drinks.

KENNEDY: Yes.

THE COURT: When did you take the last one?

KENNEDY: I would think about nine o'clock. The only way I could judge that, Your Honor, would be that I ate about ten o'clock and it was some time before I ate.

THE COURT: You had nothing alcoholic to drink after eating?

KENNEDY: No, I didn't.

THE COURT: How much liquor was at this cottage?

KENNEDY: There were several bottles, so that I wouldn't be able to tell specifically.

THE COURT: Not a large supply?

KENNEDY: I wouldn't be able to tell how much. There was an adequate supply.

THE COURT: Was there a sustained amount of drinking by the group?

KENNEDY: No, there wasn't.

THE COURT: By any particular person?

KENNEDY: Not that I noticed. There wasn't prior to the time I left.

THE COURT: Mr. Hanify, your have advised your client of his constitutional rights?

MR. HANIFY: Yes, I have, Your Honor.

THE COURT: Were you at any time that evening under the influence of alcohol?

KENNEDY: Absolutely not.

THE COURT: Did you imbibe in any narcotic drugs that evening?

KENNEDY: Absolutely not.

THE COURT: Did anyone at the party, to your knowledge?

KENNEDY: No, absolutely not.

THE COURT: In your opinion, would you be sober at the time that you operated the motor vehicle to the Dike Bridge?

KENNEDY: Absolutely sober.

Q: Senator Kennedy, what did you do immediately following your release from the automobile?

A: I was swept away by the tide that was flowing at an extraordinary rate through that narrow cut there, and was swept along by the tide and called Mary Jo's name until I was able to make my way to what would be the east side of that cut, waded up to about my waist and started back to the car, at this time was gasping and belching and coughing, went back just in front of the car. Now, the headlights of that car were still on and I was able to get to what I thought was the front of the car, although it was difficult—and I was able to identify the front of the car from the rear of the car by the lights themselves. Otherwise, I don't think I would be able to tell.

Q: How far were you swept along by the current?

A: Approximately thirty to forty feet.

Q: Did you pass under the bridge?

A: The vehicle went over the bridge on the south side and rested on the south side, and that was the direction the current was flowing, and I was swept, I would think, to the south or probably east, which would be the eastern shore of that.

Q: Some thirty feet?

A: I would think thirty to forty feet.

Q: Now, in order to get back to the car, was it necessary for you to swim?

A: I couldn't swim at that time because of the current. I waded into—swam to where I could wade, and then waded along the shore up to where I could go to the front of the car, and start diving in an attempt to rescue Mary Jo.

Q: Was the front of the car facing a westerly direction?

A: I would think it was facing in a northerly direction.

Q: Well, in regard to the bridge, could you describe the location of the automobile with relation to the bridge?

A: Well, Your Honor, in the direction of north and south, I will do the best I can.

THE COURT: We don't have any map, do we?

MR. TELLER: The bridge runs north and south, fairly close to north and south.

THE COURT: That is, coming towards Edgartown would be north and towards the ocean would be south?

MR. TELLER: Yes, sir.

MR. DINIS: May we use the chalk, Your Honor?

THE COURT: Yes, if it is helpful.

Q: Would that be helpful, Mr. Kennedy?

A: It may be.

Q: I believe there is a board behind you. Assuming the bridge is north and south—

A: Yes. [Witness draws sketch on blackboard] I would bet that the bridge runs more east-west than north-south.

MR. TELLER: Not directly north, but southeast-northwest.

(Note: It would seem someone familiar with the area ought to know the direction of the bridge.)

Q: Will you indicate, Mr. Kennedy, Edgartown?

A: I would rather have counsel draw and respond. I will be delighted to do whatever the court desires.

THE COURT: It is only for the purposes of illustration.

KENNEDY: I suppose the road runs something like this.

THE COURT: You are trying to get the relation of the car to the bridge?

MR. DINIS: Yes, Your Honor.

Q: As you went off the bridge.

A: I think it was like this.

THE COURT: All right, Mr. Dinis.

Q: Mr. Kennedy, after you emerged from the automobile, you say you were swept some 30 feet away from the car, is that correct?

A: In this direction [indicating].

Q: And how much time did it take you after you left the automobile to be swept down to about 30 feet down the river?

A: By the time I came up I was, the best estimate would be
somewhere over here, which would be probably eight to ten feet,
it is difficult for me to estimate specifically, and I think by the
time I was able at least to regain my strength, I would say it is
about thirty feet, after which time I swam in this direction until I
was able to wade, and wade back up here to this point here, and
went over to the front of the car, where the front of the car was,
and crawled over to here, dove here, and the tide would swept
[sic] out this way there, and then I dove repeatedly from this side
until, I would say, the end, and then I will be swept away the
first couple of times, again back over to this side, I would come
back again and again to this point here, or try perhaps the third
or fourth time to gain entrance to some area here until at the very
end when I couldn't hold my breath any longer, I was breathing
so heavily it was down to just a matter of seconds. I would hold
my breath and I could barely get underneath the water. I was just
able to hold on to the metal undercarriage here, and the water
itself came right out to where I was breathing and I could hold
on, I knew that I just could not get under water any more.

Q: And you were fully aware at that time of what was transpiring?

A: Well, I was fully aware that I was trying to get the girl
out of that car, and I was fully aware that I was doing everything that I possibly could to get her out of the car, and I was
fully aware at that time that my head was throbbing and my
neck was aching and I was breathless, and at that time, the last
time, hopelessly exhausted.

Q: You were not confused at that time?

A: Well, I knew that there was a girl in that car and I had to
get her out. I knew that.

Q: And you took steps to get her out?

A: I tried the best I thought I possibly could to get her out.

Q: But there was no confusion in your mind about the fact
that there was a person in the car, and that you were doing the
best you could to get that person out?

A: I was doing the very best I could to get her out.

THE COURT: My I ask you some questions here about the depth of the water?

KENNEDY: No, it was not possible to stand. The highest level of the car to the surface were the wheels and the under-carriage itself; when I held onto the undercarriage and the tide would take me down, it was up to this point [indicating].

THE COURT: You were not able to stand up at any point around any portion of that car?

KENNEDY: Yes.

Q: Mr. Kennedy, how many times, if you recall, did you make an effort to submerge and get into the car?

A: I would say seven or eight times. At the last point, the seventh or eighth attempts were barely more than five-or eight-second submersions below the surface. I just couldn't hold my breath any longer. I didn't have the strength to even come down even close to the window or the door.

Q: And do you know how much time was used in these efforts?

A: It would be difficult for me to estimate, but I would think probably fifteen to twenty minutes.

Q: And did you then remove yourself from the water?

A: I did.

Q: And how did you do that?

A: Well, in the last dive I lost contact with the vehicle again, and I started to come down this way here, and I let myself float and came over to this shore, and I came onto this shore here, and I sort of crawled and I staggered up some place in there, and was very exhausted and spent on the grass.

Q: On the west bank of the river?

A: Yes.

Q: As indicated by that chart?

A: Yes, that's correct.

Q: And how long did you spend resting?

A: Well, I would estimate probably fifteen to twenty min-utes trying to get my—I was coughing up the water and I was exhausted and I suppose the best estimate would be fifteen or twenty minutes.

Q: Now, did you say earlier that you spent fifteen or twenty minutes trying to recover Miss Kopechne?

A: That is correct.

Q: And you spent another fifteen or twenty minutes recovering on the west side of the river?

A: That is correct.

Q: Now, following your rest period, Senator, what did you do after that?

A: Well, I—

Q: You may remain seated.

A: All right. After I was able to regain my breath, I went back to the road and I started down the road, and it was extremely dark, and I could make out no forms or shapes or figures, and the only way that I could even see the path of the road was looking down the silhouette of the trees on the two sides, and I started going down that road walking, trotting, jogging, stumbling as fast as I possibly could.

Q: Did you pass any houses with lights on?

A: Not to my knowledge; never saw a cottage with a light on it.

Q: And did you then return to the cottage where your friends had been gathered?

A: That is correct.

Q: And how long did that take you to make that walk, do you recall?

A: I would say approximately fifteen minutes.

(Note: Let's see … he says he walked, stumbled, trotted and jogged some 1.2 miles … completely exhausted, in fifteen minutes … pretty fast for a man in his shape, at such a time.)

Q: And when you arrived at the cottage, as you did, is that true?

A: That is true.

Q: Did you speak to anyone there?

A: Yes, I did.

Q: And with whom did you speak?

A: Mr. Ray LaRosa.

Q: And what did you tell him?

A: I said, get me Joe Gargan.

Q: And was Joe Gargan there?

A: He was there.

Q: He was at the party?

A: Yes.

THE COURT: Excuse me a moment. Did you go inside the cottage?

KENNEDY: No, I didn't go inside.

Q: (By Mr. Dinis) What did you do? Did you sit in the automobile at that time?

A: Well, I came up to the cottage, there was a car parked there, a white vehicle, and as I came up to the back of the vehicle, I saw Ray LaRosa at the door and I said, Ray, get me Joe, and he mentioned something like, right away, and as he was going in to get Joe, I got in the back of the car.

Q: In this white car?

A: Yes.

Q: And now, did Joe come to you?

A: Yes, he did.

Q: And did you have [a] conversation with him?

A: Yes, I did.

Q: Would you tell us what the conversation was?

A: I said, you had better get Paul, too.

Q: Did you tell him what happened?

A: At that time I said, better get Paul, too.

Q: What happened after that?

A: Well, Paul came out, got into the car. I said, there has been a terrible accident, we have got to go, and we took off down the road, the Main Road there.

Q: How long had you known Mr. LaRosa prior to this evening?

A: Eight years, ten years, eight or ten years.

Q: Were you familiar with the fact or—strike that—did you have any knowledge that Mr. LaRosa had some experience in skin diving?

A: No, I never did.

Q: Now, before you drove down the road, did you make any further explanations to Mr. Gargan or Mr. Markham?

A: Before driving? No, sir. I said, there has been a terrible accident, let's go, and we took off—

Q: And they went—

A:—driving.

Q: And they drove hurriedly down?

A: That is right.

Q: Towards the Dike Bridge area.

A: That is right.

Q: And where did you finally stop the white automobile that you were riding in?

A: Mr. Gargan drove the vehicle across the bridge to some location here (indicating), and turned it so that its headlights shown over the water and over the submerged vehicle (indicating on blackboard).

Q: And what happened after the three of you arrived there?

A: Mr. Gargan and Mr. Markham took off all their clothes, dove into the water, and proceeded to dive repeatedly to try and save Mary Jo.

Q: Now, do you recall what particular time this is now when the three of you were at the—

A: I think it was at 12:20, Mr. Dinis. I believe that I looked at the Valiant's clock and believe that it was 12:20.

(Note: It was later discovered that the Valiant had no clock.)

Q: Now, Mr. LaRosa remained at the cottage?

A: Yes, he did.

Q: Was Mr. LaRosa aware of the accident?

A: No, he hadn't heard—no, I don't believe so.

Q: No one else at the cottage was told of the accident?

A: No.

Q: How many times did you go back to Dike Bridge that night?

A: Well, that was the only—

Q: After the accident, that was the only occasion?

A: The only time, the only occasion.

Q: Now, how long did Mr. Markham and Mr. Gargan remain there with you on that particular occasion?

A: I would think about forty-five minutes.

Q: And they were unsuccessful in entering the car?

A: Well, Mr. Gargan got halfway in the car. When he came out he was scraped all the way from his elbow, underneath his arm was all bruised and bloodied, and this is the one time that he was able to gain entrance, I believe, into the car itself.

Q: And did he talk to you about his experience in trying to get into the car?

A: Well, I was unable to, being exhausted, to get into the water, but I could see exactly what was happening and made some suggestions.

Q: So that you were participating in the rescue efforts?

A: Well, to that extent.

Q: You were fully aware of what was transpiring at that time?

A: Well, I was fully aware that Joe Gargan and Paul Markham were trying to get in that car and rescue that girl, I certainly would say that.

Q: Did you know at that time, or did you have any idea, how long Mary Jo had been in the water?

A: Well, I knew that some time had passed.

Q: Well, you testified earlier that you spent some fifteen or twenty minutes of—

A: Well, Mr. District Attorney, I didn't add up the time that I was adding to rescue her and time on the beach, the shore, and the time to get back and the time it took back and calculate it.

Q: Was it fair to say that she was in the water about an hour?

A: Yes, it is.

Q: Was there any effort made to call for assistance?

A: No, other than the assistance of Mr. Gargan and Mr. Markham.

Q: I know, but they failed in their efforts to recover—

A: That is right.

Q:—Miss Kopechne?

A: That is correct.

(Discussion off the record)

MR. DINIS: I believe, Your Honor, before the witness left the courtroom the question was whether or not any assistance had been asked for.

THE COURT: I think the answer had been no.

Q: (By Mr. Dinis) And now may I ask you, Mr. Kennedy, was there any reason why no additional assistance was asked for?

A: Was there any reason?

Q: Yes, was there any particular reason why you did not call either the police or the fire department?

A: Well, I intended to report it to the police.

THE COURT: That is not quite responsive to the question.

Q: Was there a reason why it did not happen at that time?

THE COURT: Call for assistance.

KENNEDY: I intended to call for assistance and to report the accident to the police within a few short moments after going back into the car.

Q: I see, and did something transpire to prevent this?

A: Yes.

Q: What was that?

A: With the court's indulgence, to prevent this, if the court would permit me I would like to be able to relate to the court the immediate period following the time that Mr. Gargan, Markham and I got back in the car.

THE COURT: I have no objection.

MR. DINIS: I have no objection.

KENNEDY: Responding to the question of the district attorney—

MR. DINIS: Yes.

KENNEDY:—at some time, I believe it was about forty-five minutes after Gargan and Marham dove, they likewise became exhausted and no further diving efforts appeared to be of any avail, and they so indicated to me, and I agreed. So they came out of the water and came back into the car and said to me, Mr. Markham and Mr. Gargan, at different times as we drove down the road towards the ferry, that it was necessary to report this accident. A lot of different thoughts came into my mind at that time, about how I was going to really be able to call Mrs. Kopechne at some time in the middle of the night to tell her that her daughter was drowned, to be able to call my own mother and my own father, relate to them, my wife, and I even—even though I knew that Mary Jo Kopechne was dead, and believe firmly that she was in the back of that car, I willed that she remained alive.

As we drove down that road I was almost looking out the front window and windows, trying to see her walking down that road. I related this to Gargan and Markham, and they said they understood this feeling, but it was necessary to report it. And about this time we came to the ferry crossing, and I got out of the car and we talked there just a few minutes.

I just wondered how all of this could possibly have happened. I also had sort of a thought and the wish and desire and the hope that suddenly this whole accident would disappear, and they reiterated that this has to be reported, and I understood at the time that I left that ferry boat, left the slip where the ferry boat was, that it had to be reported and I had full intention of reporting it, and I mentioned to Gargan and Markham something like, "You take care of the girls. I will take care of the accident," that is what I said, and I dove into the water.

Now, I started to swim out into that tide and the tide suddenly became, felt an extraordinary shove and almost pulling me down again, the water pulling me down and I suddenly realized at that time even as I failed to realize before I dove into the water that I was in a weakened condition, although as I had looked over that distance between the ferry slip and the other side, it seemed to me an inconsequential swim; but the water got colder, the tide began to draw me out, and for the second time that evening I knew I was going to drown and the strength continued to leave me. By this time, I was probably fifty yards off the shore, and I remembered being swept down toward the direction of the Edgartown Light and well out into the darkness, and I continued to attempt to swim, tried to swim at a slower pace to be able to regain whatever kind of strength that was left in me.

And some time after, I think it was about the middle of the channel, a little further than that, the tide was much calmer, gentler, and I began to get my—make some progress, and finally was able to reach the other shore, and all the nightmares and all the tragedy and all the loss of Mary Jo's death was right before me again. And when I was able to gain this shore, this Edgartown side, I pulled myself on the beach and then attempted to gain some strength.

After that, I walked up one of the streets in the direction of the Shiretown Inn.

By walking up one of the streets, I walked into a parking lot that was adjacent to the Inn and I can remember almost having no further strength to continue, and leaning against a tree for a length of time, walking through the parking lot, trying to really gather some kind of idea as to what happened and feeling that I just had to go to my room at that time, which I did by walking through the front entrance of the Shiretown Inn up the stairs.

(Note: As you are sympathetic to this sad, sad story of his miseries with little mention of the victim, note how he forgets to mention his promise to Markham and Gargan that he would immediately report the accident . . . and also, his efforts to get them to agree to a lie that would put Mary Jo in the driver's seat of the automobile. Neither of them would agree.)

Q: Do you have any idea what time you arrived at the Shiretown Inn?

A: I would say some time before two o'clock.

Q: Can you tell us now how great a distance you swam when you left the ferry slip?

A: I left just adjacent to the ferry slip here, I would say on the north side of it, and I was swept down for a number of yards and then across. I don't think I can estimate the terms of the yardage.

Q: When you arrived at the Shiretown Inn, did you talk to anyone at that time?

A: I went to my room and I was shaking with chill. I took off all my clothes and collapsed on the bed, and at this time I was very conscious of a throbbing headache, of pains in my neck, of strain on my back, but what I was even more conscious of is the tragedy and loss of a very devoted friend.

Q: Now, did you change your clothing?

A: I was unable really to determine, detect the amount of

lapse of time, and I could hear noise that was taking place. It seemed around me, on top of me, almost in the room, and after a period of time I wasn't sure whether it was morning or after-noon or nighttime, and I put on—and I wanted to find out and I put on some dry clothes that were there, a pants and a shirt, and I opened the door and I saw what I believed to be a tourist or someone standing under the light off the balcony, and asked what time it was. He mentioned to me it was, I think, 2:30, and went back into the room.

Q: Had you known Miss Kopechne prior to July the eigh-teenth?

A: Well, I have known her—my family has known her for a number of years. She has visited my house, my wife. She has visited Mrs. Robert Kennedy's house. She worked in the Robert Kennedy presidential campaign, and I would say that we have known her for a number of years.

Q: Now, directing your—

A: If the question is, have I ever been out with Mary Jo—

Q: No, that is not the question. The question was whether you just knew her socially prior to this event.

A: Well, could I give you a fuller explanation of my knowl-edge of Mary Jo, Your Honor?

MR. DINIS: I have no objection.

THE COURT: Go ahead.

KENNEDY: I have never in my life, as I have stated in my television [sic], had any personal relationship whatsoever with Mary Jo Kopechne. I never in my life have been either out with Mary Jo Kopechne, nor have I ever been with her prior to that occasion where we were not in a general assemblage of friends, associates, or members of our family.

Q: (By Mr. Dinis) Directing your attention to the nineteenth at around 7:30 a.m., did you have any conversation with anyone at that time?

A: Could I hear the question, please?

Q: The nineteenth, which was that morning at around 7:00 a.m., 7:30 a.m.—

A: Yes.

Q:—did you meet anyoe at your room?

A: Yes, I did.

Q: And whom did you meet there?

A: If Your Honor would permit me to give—I would like to be specifically responsive, and I can, I think. It might be misleading to the court if I just gave a specific response to it. Whatever the court wants.

Q: Well, the point is, what time did you get up that morning?

A: I never really went to bed that night.

Q: I see. After that noise at 2:30 in the morning, when did you first meet anyone, what time?

A: It was sometime after eight o'clock, I met the woman that was behind the counter at the Shiretown Inn, and I met Mr. Richards and Mr. Moore, very briefly Mrs. Richards, and Mr. Gargan and Mr. Markham, and I saw Mr. Tretter, but to be specifically responsive as to who I met in my room, which I believe was the earlier question, was Mr. Markham and Mr. Gargan.

Q: What time was this, sometime around eight o'clock?

A: I think it was close to 8:30.

Q: Did you have any conversation with Mr. Moore or Mrs. Moore or Mr. Richards or Mrs. Richards?

A: It is my impression that they did the talking.

Q: Well, what was that conversation, do you recall?

A: Mr. Moore was relating about how I believe some members of his crew were having difficulty with their housing arrangements.

Q: Now, what time did Mr. Markham and Mr. Gargan arrive?

A: About a few—I would think about 8:30, just a few minutes after I met Mr. Moore, probably.

Q: And do you recall how they were dressed?

A: To the best of my knowledge, a shirt and slacks.

Q: Do you recall at this time the condition of their dress?

A: Well, they had an unkempt look about it.

Q: Nothing further, nothing more than that?

A: Well, I mean, it was not pressed; it was messy looking. It was unkempt looking.

Q: Did you have any conversation with Mr. Markham or Mr. Gargan or both at that time?

A: Yes, I did.

Q: Can you give the court what the conversation was?

A: Well, they asked, had I reported the accident, and why I hadn't reported the accident; and I told them about my own thoughts and feelings as I swam across that channel and how I was always willed that Mary Jo still lived; how I was hopeful even as that night went on, and as I almost tossed and turned, paced that room and walked around that room that night, that somehow when they arrived in the morning that they were going to say that Mary Jo was still alive. I told them how I somehow believed that when the sun came up and it was a new morning, that what had happened the night before would not have happened and did not happen, and how I just couldn't gain the strength within me, the moral strength to call Mrs. Kopechne at two o'clock in the morning and tell her that her daughter was dead.

Q: Now, at some time you did call Mrs. Kopechne?

A: Yes, I did.

Q: And prior to calling Mrs. Kopechne, did you cross over on the Chappaquiddick Ferry to Chappaquiddick Island?

A: Yes, I did.

Q: And was Mr. Markham and Mr. Gargan with you?

A: Yes, they were.

Q: Now, did you then return to Edgartown after some period of time?

A: Yes, I did.

Q: Did anything prompt or cause you to return to Edgartown once you were on Chappaquiddick Island that morning?

A: Anything prompt me to? Well, what do you mean by prompt?

Q: Well, did anything cause you to return? You crossed over to Chappaquiddick?

A: Other than the intention of reporting the accident, the intention of which had been made earlier that morning.

Q: But you didn't go directly from your room to the police department?

A: No, I did not.

Q: Did you have a particular reason for going to Chappaquiddick first?

A: Yes, I did.

Q: What was that reason?

A: It was to make a private phone call to one of the dearest and oldest friends that I have, and that was to Mr. Burke Marshall. I didn't feel that I could use the phone that was available, the public phone that was available outside of the dining room at the Shiretown Inn, and it was my thought that once that I went to the police station, that I would be involved in a myriad of details, and I wanted to talk to this friend before I undertook that responsibility. (Note: Do you understand why he couldn't talk on the public phone outside the Inn based on this statement?)

Q: You mean that—

THE COURT: Excuse me, Mr. Dinis, we are now at one o'clock.

MR. DINIS: The recess.

THE COURT: I think we will take the noon luncheon recess.

(Whereupon, at 1:04 p.m., the inquest was recessed for lunch.)

AFTERNOON SESSION

THE COURT: All right, Mr. Dinis.

Q: [By Mr. Dinis] Mr. Kennedy, you said that you made a phone call to a friend, Mr. Burke Marshall?

A: I made a phone call with the intention of reaching Mr. Burke Marshall.

Q: You did not reach him?

A: No, I did not.

Q: And then, I believe, the evidence is that you left Chappaquiddick Island, crossed over on the ferry and went over to the local police department?

A: That is correct.

Q: There you made a report to Chief Arena?

A: That is right.

Q: And you arrived at the police station at approximately 10:00 a.m.?

A: I think it was sometime before 10:00.

Q: And you made a statement in writing, is that correct?

A: That's correct.

Q: Did the chief reduce this to a typewritten statement, do you know?

A: No, he did not. (Note: Chief Arena typed this statement personally).

Q: Now, I have in my hand what purports to be the statement that you made to Chief Arena at that time, and I would like to give you a copy of that, and in this statement you say—well, would you read it first, Senator?

A: Yes. That is correct.

Q: Now, Senator, prior to the phone call you made, the effort you made to contact Burke Marshall by phone, did you make any other phone calls?

A: Yes, I did.

Q: Where did you make these phone calls?

A: I made one call after eight o'clock in the morning from the public phone outside of the restaurant at the Shiretown Inn.

Q: One call?

A: That is all. This was made sometime after eight o'clock.

Q: And to whom did you make this call?

(Note: Mr. Kennedy made many more calls that he admitted to here, according to testimony and records of the New England Telephone Company, which we will cover later).

A: I was attempting to reach Mr. Stephen Smith, the party that I felt would know the number.

Q: Were you alone in the police station?

A: No. At certain times I was, but if the thrust of the question is, did I arrive at the police station with someone with me, I did.

Q: And who was that?

A: Mr. Markham.

Q: Mr. Markham?

A: Yes.

Q: With regard to the statement that you made at the police station, Senator, you wind up by saying, "When I fully realized what had happened this morning I immediately contacted the police." Now, is that in fact what you did?

THE COURT: Mr. Dinis, are you going to ask the statement be put in the record?

MR. DINIS: Yes, Your Honor.

THE COURT: Mr. Kennedy already said this was a copy of the statement he made. He already testified as to all his movements. Now, won't you let the record speak for itself?

MR. DINIS: All right, Your Honor.

THE COURT: This will be Exhibit—

MR. TELLER: Two.

THE COURT:—two.

[Statement given to Chief Arena by Senator Kennedy marked Exhibit 2]

(Note: Here is another example of the lack of investigative prosecution at this inquest).

Q: (By Mr. Dinis) Senator, you testified earlier that when you arrived at the cottage, you asked Mr. LaRosa to tell Mr. Markham you were outdoors, outside of the house, when you arrived back at the house?

A: No, that is not correct.

Q: Did you ask someone to call Mr. Markham?

A: I asked Joe Gargan, when he entered the vehicle, to call for Mr. Markham.

Q: Well, did you at that time ask anyone to take you back to Edgartown at that time, when you arrived back at the house after the accident?

A: No. I asked Mr. Gargan to go to the scene of the accident.

Q: But you didn't ask anyone to take you back directly to Edgartown?

A: I asked them to take me to Edgartown after their diving.

Q: After their diving?

A: After their diving.

Q: I show you, Mr. Kennedy, what purports to be a copy of the televised broadcast which you made approximately a week after the accident. Would you read that statement and tell me whether or not that is an exact copy of what you said?

A: [Witness complied.] Yes. After a quick reading of it, I would say that that is accurate.

MR. DINIS: Your Honor, may I introduce this statement made by Senator Kennedy in a televised broadcast?

THE COURT: You may. Exhibit number three.

Q: Now, Senator, in that televised broadcast, you said and I quote, "I instructed Gargan and Markham not to alarm Mary Jo's friends that night," is that correct?

A: That is correct. I would like to—

Q: Look at it?

A:—look at it. I believe that that is correct.

Q: It would be on page three. (Witness examined document.)

A: That is correct.

Q: Can you tell the court what prompted you to give this instruction to Markham and Gargan?

A: Yes, I can.

Q: Will you do that, please?

A: I felt strongly that if those girls were notified that an accident had taken place and that Mary Jo had in fact drowned, which I became convinced of by the time that Markham and Gargan and I left the scene of the accident, that it would only be a matter of seconds before all of those girls who were long and dear friends of Mary Jo's to go to the scene of the accident and dive themselves and enter the water and with, I felt, a good chance that some serious mishap might have occurred to any one of them. It was for that reason that I refrained—asked Mr. Gargan and Mr. Markham not to alarm the girls.

MR. DINIS: I have no further questions of Mr. Kennedy.

THE COURT: And I have no further questions. Would you be available in the event we needed you back for anything?

KENNEDY: I will make myself so available, Your Honor.

THE COURT: Well, were you planning to stay in Hyannisport or some place near?

KENNEDY: Well, I will. I will be glad to be available.

THE COURT: Otherwise, you would go back to Boston?

KENNEDY: No, I would return to Cape Cod tonight and I

would hope to be able to return to Washington sometime this week, but I would be glad to remain available to the court if the court so desired.

THE COURT: Well, it is difficult for me to say right now.

KENNEDY: Well, then, I will remain available as long as—

THE COURT: We will try to give you as much notice as possible if we felt it essential to have you back.

MR. DINIS: Your Honor, I think we could make it an overnight notice, so if the Senator had to be in Washington, we would arrange for his arrival the next day, if necessary, which may not be.

THE COURT: All right, subject to that, you are excused.

KENNEDY: Your Honor, could I talk to my counsel before being released, just on one point that I might like to address the bench on?

THE COURT: Go ahead.

(Off-the-record discussion between Mr. Kennedy and lawyers.)

(An off-the-record discussion.)

THE COURT: And I think we can put in the record this question. Why did you not seek further assistance after Mr. Markham and Mr. Gargan had exhausted their efforts in attempting to reach Mary Jo? Now, you give the answer.

KENNEDY: It is because I was completely convinced at that time that no further help and assistance would do Mary Jo any more good. I realized that she must be drowned and still in the car at this time, and it appeared the question in my mind at that time was, what should be done about the accident.

THE COURT: Anything further? Off the record.

(Discussion of the record.)

THE COURT: All right, take this.

KENNEDY: Since the alcoholic intake is relevant, there is one further question, Your Honor, and although I haven't been asked it, I feel that in all frankness and fairness and for a complete record that it should be included as a part of the complete proceedings, and that is that during the course of the race that afternoon, that there were two other members of my crew and I shared what would be two beers between us at different points in the race, and one other occasion in which there was some modest intake of alcohol would be after the race at the slip in which Ross Richards' boat was attached, moored, that I shared a beer with Mr. John Driscoll. The sum and substance of that beer would be, I think, less than a quarter of one, but I felt that for the complete record that at least the court should at least be aware of these instances as well.

THE COURT: Anything more?

KENNEDY: There is nothing further.

THE COURT: Anything more, Mr. Dinis?

MR. DINIS: No, Your Honor.

THE COURT: All right, you are excused subject to further recall. Off the record.

(Discussion off the record.)

THE COURT: All right, your next witness, Mr. Dinis.

MR. DINIS: Mr. Malloy of the phone company.

THE COURT: Ask the officer to bring him in.

(While you may wonder why we chose to provide the complete testimony of the Senator, we think it important for you to realize the changes in his story from the original statement to this testimony, and, to understand how low-key the district attorney was in questioning the Senator . Certainly, in today's justice system, this simple questioning would never have sufficed—nor would the inconsistencies in his testimony.)

CHAPTER 10

TELEPHONE COMPANY TESTIMONY

Testifying for the New England Telephone Company were Charles R. Parrott and Robert Malloy.

MR. DINIS: Mr. Malloy, would you please take the witness stand?

MR. PARROTT: I represent the New England Telephone Company today.

MR. DINIS: Are you an attorney?

MR. PARROTT: Yes, I am an attorney.

THE COURT: Have you filed an appearance?

MR. PARROTT: Not as of—not yet, Your Honor.

THE COURT: I wish you would do so. Were you here this morning?

MR. PARROTT: Yes, Your Honor, I was.

A: ROBERT MALLOY, Sworn

EXAMINATION BY MR. DINIS:

Q: Your name, please?

A: A. Robert Malloy.

Q: And your legal address?

A: Thirty-seven Alba Road, Wellesley Hills.

Q: And are you employed by the New England Telephone Company?

A: That is correct.

Q: In what capacity?

A: I am general accounting supervisor in Massachusetts.

Q: Now, in regard to a summons directed to John O'Connor, and, by the way, what is Mr. O'Connor's position with the phone company?

A: He currently is a commission manager in Hyannis.

Q: I see. Did you bring with you, as a result of that summons, records of telephone calls made with a credit card of Edward M. Kennedy on July eighteenth and nineteenth, 1969?

A: I did, sir.

Q: Do you have those records with you?

A: Yes, I do.

Q: Would you produce those records at this time?

A: Yes.

THE COURT: This doesn't mean one single thing if the name of the witness doesn't appear.

MR. PARROTT: Fine, Your Honor, I will add it on.

Q: Now, in response to my inquiry, did you tell me that Edward M. Kennedy had more than one credit card?

A: The information that I have on credit cards that are billed through Senator Kennedy's accounts are, in one case, there were more than one billed to a single account, yes, sir.

THE COURT: You are talking about the number of cards?

MR. DINIS: Yes, the number of accounts he has.

THE WITNESS: I was able to investigate three of his accounts, one in Boston, one in Washington and one in Virginia, and the cards, the original records that I do have, is the information that originated in the New England area. I do not have the original records of calls that originated in, let me say, New Jersey, Maryland.

THE COURT: I still don't get this clear. Mr. Kennedy had more than one credit card?

THE WITNESS: No, sir.

THE COURT: He had one credit card from the telephone company?

THE WITNESS: No. To explain it, in Boston he has a billing account, telephone account, and there were, I think, six or seven cards assigned to that account. Now, it does not necessarily have to be in the name of Senator Kennedy, the card itself, but it is billed to his accounts.

THE COURT: Tell me the distinction between what I show you and what you are trying to explain to me, that I frankly at the moment do not understand. I have a credit card. It has a specific number. When I call I give that number?

THE WITNESS: Yes.

THE COURT: The charge is then made to me on my telephone?

THE WITNESS: Appears on your bill.

THE COURT: Now, could I have more than one credit card?

THE WITNESS: Yes, you could.

THE COURT: Charged to two different telephones?

THE WITNESS: Two different telephones, or you could have more charged to that one. In that case, we go into a different kind of series that come up in billing.

THE COURT: The card that you are referring to is the evidence of the account?

THE WITNESS: That is right. It is billed against the Senator 's account in Boston.

THE COURT: We are now talking about accounts in his name and his name alone?

THE WITNESS: Yes, sir.

MR. DINIS: Now, with regard to your records, do they show any calls emanating from Chappaquiddick or Edgartown?

A: Yes, they do, sir.

Q: Will you produce the records that show those specific calls emanating from Edgartown or Chappaquiddick for those particular dates, July eighteenth and nineteenth?

A: (Witness complied.)

MR. PARROTT: If I may address the court at this point, Your Honor, there is some primary evidence, if you will, or [sic] basic cards that are made by the telephone operator at the time the call is placed. Mr. Malloy has just about all of these with him, as to calls originating in the New England area of the New England Telephone and Telegraph. To assist the court, he has made a compilation of those which I think would be helpful. He puts them all together, and puts them in their chronological time sequence from July eighteenth to July nineteenth. It may save Your Honor time to look at that list rather than go through each individual card.

THE COURT: All right.

Q: Would you explain this sheet showing the calls that were made as to what times of the day they were made?

A: Yes, sir. Like this first one—

Q: On the eighteenth?

A: On the eighteenth, was made at 10:08 a.m. and it lasted for one minute and 20 seconds. That was a call from Edgartown. (Note: Kennedy said he didn't arrive until one p.m.)

Q: To Arlington, Virginia?

A: To Arlington, Virginia.

Q: That this was made at 12:30 p.m. that day?

A: That is right.

Q: This at 6:39 p.m.?

A: That evening, yes, sir. On the nineteenth, the first one at 10:57.

Q: Would there be a difference there, with regard to the calling locations as to Vineyard Haven and Edgartown?

A: Yes. The calls at office 627 is Edgartown. Six-nine-three is Vineyard Haven, and each location has at least one, if not many, different central outlets, depending upon the density of the population.

Q: And that call lasted 23 minutes?

A: Twenty-three minutes and 54 seconds, sir.

Q: And it began at 10:57?

A: Yes, sir.

Q: Now, this is on the morning—

A: On the morning of [the] nineteenth, sir.

THE COURT: Isn't this thing self-explanatory?

MR. DINIS: Well, I don't know, Your Honor. It is not difficult.

THE COURT: Right now, somebody is going to have to teach me what it means. Would you just let me look at it? Time made, length of call, originated from 627 and 693 with which I am very familiar, and it gives the town from which the call came. What does CO mean?

THE WITNESS: That is the central office from which the phone call originated, sir.

THE COURT: What about the area code?

THE WITNESS: No area code that I indicate, sir. Arlington, Virginia, would be a separate one. Washington would be another one.

THE COURT: Oh, I see. You have got a term location?

THE WITNESS: Yes, sir, and the party to which the phone was listed.

THE COURT: "A" means a.m.?

THE WITNESS: Yes, sir.

THE COURT: "P" means p.m.?

THE WITNESS: Yes, sir.

THE COURT: I ask this question now. You do not require the person initiating the call to identify himself or herself?

THE WITNESS: No, sir.

THE COURT: In other words, anyone can use my credit card if they know the number?

THE WITNESS: Yes, sir.

THE COURT: Do you want to offer this as an exhibit?

MR. DINIS: Well, Your Honor, I don't see any harm in offering it for the record.

THE COURT: It doesn't, at the moment, tell me anything.

MR. DINIS: No, it doesn't, and it may not, but we will make it part of the record.

THE COURT: Exhibit number four, I believe.

(Compilation of list of telephone numbers marked exhibit four)

MR. DINIS: Thank you, gentlemen. There will be no further questions. Thank you very much for your assistance.

(Witness excused.)

"Boiler Room" girls stayed here.

CHAPTER 11

DETECTIVE FLYNN AND "A CURRENT AFFAIR"

Bernie Flynn, a state police lieutenant detective assigned to the investigation, was interviewed years later on Maury Povich's show *A Current Affair*. Flynn said,

"My immediate feeling when Ted Kennedy went on TV to explain what had happened, explain his situation and his feelings . . . my immediate reaction was, this guy is lying. I felt sorry for him. His two brothers were killed. He was getting bad advice. So, I contacted Kennedy's brother-in-law, Stephen Smith.

"I called Stephen Smith at about two o'clock in the afternoon at his office. I talked to him very rapidly ... that I was interested in helping Senator Ted Kennedy. He told me to call him at his home that evening. And I did. He suggested I talk with Herbert Miller. Everyone calls him Jack. He's an attorney in Washington, D.C. I told him I'm going down to Washington, D.C. in a couple of days, I've got a case I'm working on. I asked if that would be a good time to call him. And he said yes.

"I did go down, and I contacted Jack Miller at his office. He told me to stay at the airport, and directed me to a particular lounge. He arrived in about twenty minutes."

Flynn then had another meeting with both Miller and Stephen Smith, this time at Logan Airport in Boston. He told the two of them that there was no more information available, and that Kennedy could walk into the inquest and not worry about being asked any questions that he might be unprepared for.

Throughout the inquest, various witnesses gave testimony that contradicted each other's statements, as well as those of the Senator . Yet the district attorney and the judge seemed content to leave all these discrepancies alone. However, at the end of the inquest, Judge James A. Boyle found the following:

1) that Kennedy and Kopechne did not intend to drive to the ferry slip and that it was probable that Kennedy was aware of the Dike Bridge hazard; and,

2) that there was probable cause to believe that Edward M. Kennedy had operated his vehicle negligently, and that such operation appears to have contributed to the death of Mary Jo Kopechne. By finding this probable cause, Judge Boyle could have issued a warrant for the arrest of the person charged with the commission of a crime. Obviously, he did not.

Kennedy's reaction: I reject these findings. Apparently, that rejection was enough to stop the D.A. from taking the case any further. Of course, Dinis never had any intention of calling for a grand jury investigation. The inquest was ridiculous, inasmuch as an inquest does not have the power to indict. All it can do is recommend to the D.A. that it is advisable to convene a grand jury. A grand jury can deem that a crime was committed, and accused the parties suspected of such crime.

Les Leland, however, refused to give up. "I think and feel strongly that Kennedy was given preferential treatment from the beginning. Remember, we used to put presidents, Senators and representatives above reproach. Whatever they said was pretty much gospel. We put these people on a pedestal. They were God-like to many citizens.

"Chief Arena took everything at face value. Things would have been different if it happened today. This happened before Watergate. If it happened now, there would have been more investigative reporting. Questions would have been asked. There would have been more investigation. They would have secured the area. They would not have flown the body off the island as quickly as they did. They would have demanded an autopsy. They would have done more testing at the scene. A lot of things have changed over the years. They are now exploring every angle, turning over every leaf. That wasn't done in this case. The grand jury would have been able to subpoena witnesses. Ask hard questions. There wouldn't have been an inquest. Especially a secret one. Hadn't been used for years and years and years. Kennedy's people were able to change the rules. They made it a secretive hearing, when originally it was to be an open investigative hearing."

CHAPTER 12

THE GRAND JURY

In October of 1969, Dinis spoke to the jurors during a regularly scheduled session. He was, as one juror stated, "full of fire and brimstone." He told the jury he was out to get Kennedy.

He reportedly said, "It didn't matter how much money he had or how much power, we were going to uncover the truth." Dinis told the panel that the body of Mary Jo would be exhumed, and an autopsy and an inquest held. And, if need be, he was going to call the grand jury back. He then recessed the jury. That was the end of his involvement, because he refused to reconvene the grand jury. He stated that a judge should take charge of the investigation, not him.

Dinis was probably performing for the press and the public, but as Leland had said, "Dinis made it clear that he had no intention of bringing the case before a grand jury."

Les Leland, then age 29, was trying to build his new business at the pharmacy, as well as raise his family. He didn't have the time, the inclination, or the knowledge to call the grand jury to investigate the case. He constantly talked with District Attorney Dinis, telling him he was the one with the knowledge to call the grand jury. He was the one who knew what to do. But Leland's effort continuously fell on deaf ears.

Leland's pharmacy license expires on the last day of every year. "The state sends you an automatic renewal—like they do a drivers' license. You get it in the mail. You fill it out and send the check off. I never received the renewal notification. I never got it. Never thought about it. One of those things you never think about. As I said, I never received it, so I get a phone call early in the morning on December thirty-first from a young lady who identifies herself as an employee of the Massachusetts State Pharmacy Board of Registration. She informs me that the state police have been instructed to be at my pharmacy the next morning to padlock my doors.

"I asked if I could send up a check immediately, and she responded that she had to have it in hand by the close of business that day. She also asked me not to mention this call to anyone, or she would lose her job. The young lady informed me that all the paperwork would be ready, just come into the office, and identify yourself, and that you want to renew your pharmacy license to conduct a retail pharmacy business.

"I was frantic. What was I supposed to do? Here it was New Years Eve day. How was I going to get to Boston? Could I take the ferry, drive and get to Boston in enough time? Was there a flight I could get directly to Boston? I was running around, as they say, 'like a chicken with its head cut off.' Finally, I checked the plane schedules and found a flight I could make that would get me there in time.

"I ran home, changed clothes, drove to the airport and got there just in time to catch the plane to Boston. I was a nervous wreck. I was on the plane, but I still had to get there before the office closed, which I knew would be early because of the holiday. We landed and I rushed off the plane, ran through the airport and grabbed a cab to the State Pharmacy Board office. I arrived about three p.m., just as they were getting ready to close. I introduced myself to a female clerk and handed her my check for the license fee. She smiled. I thanked her and left with my license renewal in hand. I thought it was just a coincidence. One of those administrative glitches that just happens. I never connected it to my position as foreman, or the entire grand jury situation."

Leland, however, could not give up his quest to discover what had really happened at Chappaquiddick that night in July. How much truth and how much fiction was involved in the Senator's story? In spite of the problems he was encountering and the lack of cooperation he was receiving, he knew an investigation was necessary.

"I felt we owed it to the people to delve into what really happened. It had been too long since the girl died. A great injustice had been done. There's been a whitewash, a cover up, and things have been swept under the rug. It's time the public found out what really happened. We owed it to the Kopechnes, who when informed of the death of their daughter by Kennedy were unaware that Kennedy was the driver of the car. The inquest was a travesty. The Kopechnes weren't allowed to attend the inquest. The grand jury wasn't allowed to know what happened, or the results of the inquest. Kennedy was treated with kid gloves. The charges against him weren't even what were demanded in a case of this nature. It was unjust, and I was left no alternative but to open a grand jury investigation."

Here's where the party took place.

CHAPTER 13

DECISION TIME

Leland said, "I agonized for weeks after the inquest transcript was impounded. Dinis implied in our conversations that the jury would find the inquest judge's opinions very interesting. The D.A. was constantly baiting me to be the one to call the grand jury back into special session.

"I had to get away. I took my wife and two sons to Florida for a two-week vacation. It gave me plenty of time, without any distractions to think about my duties as foreman.

"I mentioned to my Dad that I was seriously considering reconvening the grand jury. My Dad, who had been a Selectman for many years, told me, 'You better leave this alone and walk away. You are dealing with the biggest, most powerful political machine in the country. The Kennedys will destroy you if you continue.'

"Powerful words. But, then I didn't always listen to Dad."

When Leland returned to Martha's Vineyard, he contacted Dinis to find out how and who to contact in order to re-convene the grand jury.

Leland knew he was in over his head, but he felt the need to get on with it. On St. Patrick's Day, March 17, 1970, he prepared a letter to Chief Justice Joseph Tauro of the Superior Court, asking that the grand jury be called out of recess to review the accident at Chappaquiddick. He wrote that the grand jury had "a duty and a responsibility to come up with answers that have been long overdue, and try to close the case once and for all."

"I sent the letter registered, with return receipt requested. The only other person aware that I sent this letter was District Attorney Dinis.

"A few days after sending the letter, I received a call at the pharmacy from one of the news media. The reporter told me he had heard from a reliable source that I had sent a letter to the chief justice requesting that the grand jury be reconvened. Obviously, that 'reliable source' had to be Ed Dinis.

"I told him yes, I did send the letter. That call came at about nine a.m. Within an hour or two I received another call, this one from one of the local TV stations. This caller told me he had contacted the Superior Court, and they acknowledged that no letter had been received from a Leslie Leland.

"I was angered and frustrated. I told the media that I was holding in my hand the receipt signed by the judge's office. Again, the media contacted the judge's office, and they still denied having received the letter.

"That same TV station came to the pharmacy some time around noon that day and interviewed me. I showed them the signed return receipt. They left the pharmacy and returned to Boston, notifying me that the interview would be seen on the six o'clock news.

"At about five p.m. that evening I received a call from the TV station, telling me they were not going to air the interview. They said they got a call from the judge's office stating the letter had just been received. No explanations were given as to what happened to the letter for all those days after it was received and signed for.

"The cover-up is all around. My father's words were more right than wrong."

CHAPTER 14

THE THREATS

Shortly after calling for the grand jury to convene, Les received the first of several communications.

As Leland recalls, "I was at the pharmacy one morning, when one of the pharmacists told me I had a phone call. I picked up the phone and said 'good morning.' I heard this gruff voice on the line say, 'Is this Leland?' I said yes. Then I heard him say, 'Let me tell you something, Leland, you had better cancel your plans to call the grand jury.'

"I asked, 'Who is this?' He repeated his statement about the grand jury, and I said something like, 'What, are you nuts?'

"He then raised his voice and said, 'I'm not nuts, and you better listen to what I say. I told you not to call the grand jury. And, if you think I'm kidding, you're not going to like what will happen to your wife and kids if you go through with this. I don't think you want them hurt, so I'm giving you this warning. We don't play games. So, get it done and get it done quick, or we're going to have to do things you're not going to like.'

"Then I asked, 'Is this some kind of joke or something?'

"He replied, 'Believe me, this is no joke and I'm not kidding. There are people who don't want this grand jury, and they are willing to make sure it don't happen. So I'm giving you this warning. And I strongly suggest you take it. 'Cause I know you don't want anything to happen to your wife and kids.' Then he hung up."

Leland was shook up, to say the least. But he couldn't believe that phone call was for real. The more he thought about it, the more he was sure this was someone trying to pull his leg … a crank call. After all, the voice and the conversation sounded like something out of a Humphrey Bogart or Jimmy Cagney movie.

Leland debated whether or not to tell his wife, the police or some of his friends about the call, but decided against it. He still thought it must have been some whacko or prankster, getting his jollies off. Then he recalled the situation with the pharmacy license. Are the two related? he wondered. The more he pondered what had happened, the more confused he became. It was constantly on his mind. Interfering with his work routine and his family life … what to do? That was almost all he could think about, yet he kept it to himself. Why have others worry? he thought. It doesn't make sense.

A few evenings later, Leland was spending some family time when the phone rang. He answered it, said hello and heard:

"Is this the Leland residence?"

"Yes," he said.

"Is this Mr. Leslie Leland?"

"Yes, and who is this?

"Mr. Leland, several days ago you received a call from a friend of mine. He suggested that you call off the grand jury investigation and described to you what might happen if you didn't. Do you recall that conversation?"

"Yes, I recall it … but, who is this? I want to know who is calling or I'm going to hang up."

"I wouldn't hang up Mr. Leland. It doesn't matter who I am. I am calling because I want to help you. I don't want to see any harm come to you or your family. But, if you don't do what my friend told you to do, I am afraid there will be nothing I can do. So, think of it this way. I am a good Samaritan trying to save you from more trouble than you have ever known or would want to know—"

"Wait a minute," Leland said, "I am tired of these threats—"

"Don't interrupt me, Mr. Leland. As I tried to tell you, I am trying to alleviate a problem that could ruin your life. It's very simple. Call off the grand jury investigation and all will be forgotten. My friend asked you before and you didn't act. Now I'm asking you again. You can get on with your pharmacy business and your family life. You won't hear anything further from my friend, which, believe me, will be a blessing for all of you. It's as simple as that. *Comprende?* With that I'll say good night, and I hope you have a wonderful evening."

Les recalled: "Now it really hit me. These guys weren't kidding. What was so strange was the different tones in the phone calls. The first caller was very gruff. The type of voice you'd hear from a gangster in the movies. The second was very calm and sophisticated. Completely different. Like a Jekyll-and-Hyde scenario.

"I was shook up. I didn't know what to do. I was at a loss. So, after we put the kids to bed that night, I told my wife about what had happened. The license situation and two phone calls. She said, 'Forget the grand jury. Who cares? Let Kennedy get away with it unscathed.' I listened intensively, but knew there was no way I could let it drop. I knew the investigation had to go on. Too many people, the public, the Kopechnes ... they had to know. I had been receiving letters from all over the world. Letters demanding that the cause of this accident be determined. I would say that 99 percent of the letters felt that he was guilty. My answer was that I was not going to call off the investigation, but I was going to contact the state police for protection."

Leland contacted the police and told them about the phone calls. They agreed to provide protection for his family and himself. He said it made him feel a lot safer. Though he was still scared, he would not let it deter him from reconvening the grand jury. There were other threatening calls, but they were not answered because Leland was away from home. One call came on the day before the grand jury reconvened. State Police Chief Charles Harrington answered it. He was at the Leland home investigating the threats, and answered the phone when it rang. Harrington said the caller hung up when he recognized that the voice was not Leland's.

"I don't want to sound like a hero, because I'm not," said Leland, "but I just couldn't let a girl's death be swept under the rug, so to speak, because of the political influence of the man who supposedly drove the car into the pond accidentally."

About a week later, Leland received a letter at home renewing the previous threats from the two phone calls, the same threats to the well-being of his family and himself. He turned this letter over to the state police. With this further proof, the police intensified their protection. Leland could go nowhere without being accompanied by the police. It made him feel safer, but uncomfortable.

"I really appreciated everything the state police did. They were great in watching over us. But it is still hard to get used to someone watching your every move all day and all night long. I don't think you can really understand the feeling unless you personally experience it."

CHAPTER 15

GRAND JURY RECONVENES

Superior Court Chief Justice Tauro granted the request to reconvene the Dukes County grand jury. Judge Tauro's written reply stated: "By reason of your request this day received that the grand jury for Dukes Country be reconvened on Monday, April 6, 1970, the chief justice has directed the sheriff of Dukes County that he cause the grand jury to be assembled in Edgartown on that day at 10 a.m."

Further, he wrote that he would assign a Superior Court judge "to preside at a criminal sitting of the court at Edgartown" and that judge would "instruct the grand jury and receive its returns of true bills or no bills."

Note: It is important to know that under Massachusetts law, the grand jury has the power to ask questions and call any witnesses it desires, and to view any documents, impounded or not.

Judge Wilfred J. Paquet was assigned to preside at the reconvening of the grand jury. He had been presiding at the first session of the Suffolk Superior Criminal Court in Boston. During this session, Judge Paquet was acting on petitions filed by the Senator and others seeking to examine the impounded documents relating to the inquest held into the death of Mary Jo Kopechne.

There had been much speculation that Judge Paquet was very patronizing to the Kennedys based on the backing they had given him over the years. He had been a member of the state Democratic committee, and was awarded his judgeship after he managed a successful campaign for the governor. His ability to preside in a fair and equitable manner was clearly questionable. As one source stated, the judge was a "Kennedyphile."

Leland was outspoken in his efforts to reconvene the grand jury. He had been interviewed years later on several TV and radio shows, including *A Current Affair* and *Geraldo*. He continually reiterated his desire to get to the truth. As he said many times, "The public is entitled to know, and the Kopechnes should have closure as to the death of their daughter." Before proceeding, he polled the grand jury, and all members agreed to reconvene. "The other members were supportive. They, too, wanted to get to the truth. I had told them that the district attorney said that we would find the transcripts very interesting, as well as the remarks of Judge Boyle at the end of the inquest. The statements made by Kennedy and those made by the girls and others just wouldn't mesh. There would be different stories with different versions and time frames. Dinis didn't say we couldn't see them; just that we would find them interesting."

When his request to reconvene the grand jury was granted, Leland said, "Dinis will be my legal counsel, but I'm going to conduct it myself."

Leland arrived at the courthouse the morning of April 6, slightly before 10 a.m. Captain Harrington and a few troopers from the Middleboro state police barracks accompanied him. As he climbed to the top of the stairs of the courthouse, Dinis met him. Without so much as a greeting, Dinis blurted out, "The judge is seriously considering holding you in contempt of court."

"I was shocked by the statement and the coldness of his approach," Leland said. "I was intimidated. I was fearful, but also angered and disgusted with the judicial system. Especially Dinis and Paquet. After he hit me with that statement, I asked him just what basis would the judge have to hold me in contempt. Then Dinis told me to be quiet, stop talking so much and get into the jury room. He told me that the judge felt I was talking too much and answering too many questions from the press, that I had no right to speak publicly."

Leland described how the jury entered the room. For starters, the judge ordered Reverend Donald Couza of St. Elizabeth's Church to deliver a prayer. In his opening, the Reverend prayed "that prejudice be set aside and replaced by justice and charity."

Then Paquet began his long tirade on how the jury should perform. "He preached at us for what seemed to be an eternity. Actually, it lasted more than an hour. He started out by saying he would tolerate neither noise nor interference of any sort with his instructions to the jury. He directed statements to the press, demanding that no recording devices be allowed in the courtroom. He threatened the members of the press with warnings that anyone using these devices would be dealt with by the court.

"He told us there were three things the jury must understand under the oath we took. Those were diligent inquiry, secrecy, and impartiality. 'You are both the sword' he said, 'and the shield of justice. The sword is the terror of the crime and the shield is the protection of the innocent against unlawful accusations.'"

Paquet went on to explain that the function of the grand jury is to indict those people the jury believes may have committed a crime, and that the jury was not accountable to anyone but the court itself.

"Nobody can be prosecuted for a crime, except by the vote of a grand jury," Paquet continued. "But you must bear in mind that you will not be trying this case. You decide on an indictment strictly on the evidence submitted. If anyone approaches the grand jury and attempts to influence your vote, you must notify the court. I will not tolerate any interference with the grand jury. I will deal with it summarily as contempt of court."

Leland also recalls the judge then explaining that at least twelve members of the jury had to vote for any indictment, and that the foreman must sign the indictment even if he does not totally agree with it.

"I also recall him saying that we could return an indictment for perjury if we believed that any of the information from sources indicated that one of the witnesses had lied under oath," Leland continued. "We were all somewhat shook up, almost fearful, when he sternly told us, in no uncertain terms, everything that goes on in the jury room must be kept silent. Forever."

From the reports of the press, Paquet went on, "Whatever you hear in the grand jury room from witnesses, or whatever the district attorney says to you, or whatever your fellows might say, you must keep secret.

"If you reveal one single thing that happens in the grand jury room it will be a violation—and I don't mean just for a day, but forever that your lips must be sealed; also the lips of the prosecuting officer, the reporter, or the interpreter, if one is used.

"And the reason for this is that the grand jury hears only one side of the case."

There was no doubt to the jury that Judge Paquet was in absolute charge. Undoubtedly, that was what he intended them to believe when he declared, "Control of a grand jury is complete, and neither the grand jury nor the prosecutor can seek review by another court."

Leland and the other jurors wanted to call witnesses who had testified at the inquest, but the judge actually told the jurors they were not allowed to subpoena anyone who had already testified.

"This really upset me," related Leland, "as the key people involved had all been brought in to give testimony at the inquest. When we went into the juror's room, I immediately asked Dinis about calling Kennedy, Markham, Gargan and the five girls who were in Chappaquiddick with Mary Jo. District Attorney Dinis, who was counsel to the grand jury, in no uncertain terms reiterated what Judge Paquet had said. He said he wouldn't call these witnesses because the investigation he conducted prior to the inquest and during the inquest was more than sufficient. He further said he wouldn't call anyone who has already been called, and he wouldn't redo work that has already been done."

When the jury asked Mr. Dinis to request that the judge call the witnesses, they were told that the judge agreed with the District Attorney's assessment. Anyone who had previously testified could not be called by the grand jury.

Leland and the other jurors then huddled, and decided that if they couldn't call witnesses from the inquest, they wanted to see the transcripts of the witnesses' testimony from the inquest. Leland went to Dinis with this request. After a few brief moments of conversation, Dinis directed Leland to go to the judge's chambers. Leland left the juror's room and walked next door.

"I walked into the judge's chambers somewhat sheepishly," Leland explained. "As I came in, the judge's head was looking down at something on his desk. I said, 'Your Honor, as foreman of the grand jury, I have been asked to request that the members of the jury be allowed to see and read the transcripts of all the testimony from the inquest into the death of Mary Jo Kopechne, because we are not being allowed to call witnesses from the inquest.' I don't think I'll ever forget the look on his face as he looked up at me for a second, then stared down at a piece of paper in front of him. If looks could kill, it'd be all over. Done. Finished. He read from this prepared statement, letting me know that the transcripts of testimony from the inquest were impounded and would remain that way until after the grand jury had been dismissed. Based on the mood in the room, I thought it best not to inquire any further into the matter, or ask any questions or make any statements.

"I left the judge's chambers, went back to the jury and told them what had happened. We discussed what we should do and what choices we had. Should we just forget it, or should we call witnesses that did not testify at the inquest? After some heated debate, we decided to move forward, though none of us was convinced that this direction would prove beneficial in getting to the bottom of the mystery."

Senator Kennedy stayed here during Regatta

CHAPTER 16

DAY ONE AND TWO, SESSIONS

During the afternoon session of the first day of the grand jury investigation, two witnesses were called. The first was Stephen Gentle, owner and manager of the Edgartown airport; the other was Mrs. Nina Trott, as reservations manager at the Shiretown Inn where Kennedy stayed. Each testified for about ten minutes. Mr. Gentle stated that he was unaware of any mysterious flights from his grass-strip airport during the early hours July 19. Mrs. Trott said she had quit work about midnight and had not seen the Senator return from Chappaquiddick. The jury then recessed until the following morning.

The next morning, two other witnesses testified. Benjamin Hall, projectionist at Ye Olde Town House Photoplays (the local movie theater), was summoned because he lived across the street from the Shiretown Inn and might have seen Kennedy return to the hotel after he had supposedly swam across the channel. Next witness was Robert J. Carroll, former Democratic Selectman and part owner of the Harbor View Hotel. He was called because of rumors that he had flown Kennedy off the island in the early morning after the accident to Hyannis Port on Cape Cod, and then flown him back to Martha's Vineyard. Kennedy had a summer home at Hyannis Port. Carroll said the rumors were ridiculous.

After the two witnesses testified the morning of April 7, Leland called the grand jury together to discuss the tactics for possible further investigation. The jury agreed there were many aspects of the case that troubled them. To start with, why did Kennedy, who was familiar with the island, take a wrong turn? Why did it take him nine or ten hours to report the accident? Why didn't he seek help from the homes near the accident scene that had lights on? Exactly what went on during the nine or ten hours before he finally reported the accident? Why was Ms. Kopechne's body embalmed before an autopsy was held? Why was the inquest into her death held in secrecy, and the inquest report kept under wraps for months?

Following a great deal of discussion, the jury decided to end the investigation. "We were stymied by our inability to call important witnesses, and to be allowed to read the inquest report. The witnesses we were able to call could not provide any information that was truly relevant to the case," Leland said.

Shortly before 11 a.m., the jury appeared before Judge Paquet. The judge asked the foreman if the jury had any presentments. "I rose from my seat and said, 'I have no presentments,'" said Leland. A presentment is the jury's declaration of an offense. "I then sat down. The judge immediately sternly snapped in a harsh, scolding voice, 'Mr. Foreman, stand up.'

"I stood immediately and the judge again snapped, ' Does the grand jury, not you, have any presentments?' I then said somewhat sheepishly that 'We, the grand jury, had no presentments.'"

The judge then thanked the jury and dismissed them. Many of the jury members were angry because they were unable to perform their job adequately. They complained that vital evidence had been kept from them and they were stopped from doing any meaningful investigation. "It was a cover-up from beginning to end," stated Leland.

Leland said that other jurors, under agreements of anonymity, said they wanted to call the undertaker who claimed he'd tried to get Dr. Donald Mills to change his medical finding that Mary Jo died of drowning. Another wanted to call a boater who claimed to have heard some friends of the Senator talking in a boat as they crossed the channel, conflicting with Kennedy's statement that he swam the channel. The district attorney said it was hearsay evidence.

Another juror said she felt frustrated by the whole experience. Still another stated that he didn't mind that they couldn't call the Senator as a witness because "Senators always lie anyways." They all agreed that they were allowed to ask a lot of questions, but were only allowed to discuss issues brought up by the judge or district attorney, or from personal knowledge.

One juror said, "The whole thing was a whitewash. I felt there was too much money and power involved. It was frustrating and disillusioning for all the grand jury members. We had no evidence to work with. Our purpose was to find the truth, but we found ourselves blocked in every direction we turned. A grand jury's not supposed to be restricted in any way, but we were. This makes me angry. But we don't like to say much about it. We live in Massachusetts, and we're scared. The Kennedy's have a lot of power."

Finally, a juror concluded, "The whole thing was a whitewash and a cover-up. We were made to look like idiots. Every avenue we pursued became a dead end. We were completely demoralized at the end."

Leland added, "The grand jury does have the right to subpoena anyone. Also, we had the right to read the inquest transcripts. I became aware of these rights six to eight months after the grand jury was shut down.

"I had many lawyers come to me after the grand jury proceedings with this information. This knowledge brought up all the emotions again of betrayal, of being used and manipulated by the judge and district attorney. But we were sworn to secrecy for life."

In his book *Senatorial Privilege*, Leo Damore quoted juror Theresa Morse. It was undoubtedly the most direct, profound and damning statement any member of the grand jury had made. She said, "A bigger bunch of dumbbells you'd never hope to find—I most certainly include myself. We were dupes and boobs, and let ourselves be manipulated. Nobody ever briefed us properly about what we could do. We were a powerful body made impotent by Mr. Dinis."

Years later, the *National Enquirer* interviewed District Attorney Dinis. He admitted that he had kept testimony given at Mary Jo's inquest away from the jurors, and refused to call witnesses who had testified at the inquest.

Dinis went on, "Upon my own responsibility as district attorney, I felt that the investigation we conducted prior to the inquest and during the inquest was more than sufficient. I told the jurors I will not call anyone who has been called as a witness at the inquest. And I won't go over the work that's already been done."

He added, "Where the grand jury was eager to investigate this case, state and county officials were not. No one wanted this case, and everyone kept shuffling it around like a hot potato."

Dinis later admitted that had he let the grand jury proceed in a manner that was not in keeping with normal custom and procedure. If the grand jury had not been restricted in their efforts, "there is no doubt that they would have come in with an indictment of Ted Kennedy for involuntary manslaughter." It is interesting to note that Dinis, though heavily favored, lost the next election in his bid for his fourth term as district attorney.

Chapter 17

Frustration

Leslie Leland was frustrated, and remains so to this day.

"Chief Arena took everything at face value. Things would have been different if it happened today. This happened before Watergate. If it happened now there would have been more investigative reporting. Tough questions would have been asked. More investigation. They would have secured the area. More investigation. They would not have flown the body off the island as quickly as they did. They would have demanded an autopsy. They would have done more testing at the scene.

"A lot of things have changed over the years. We've seen it change. O.J. is an excellent example. The media and law enforcement are now exploring every angle, turning over every leaf. That wasn't done in this case.

"Today, the grand jury would have been able to subpoena witnesses. Ask hard questions. There wouldn't have been an inquest, especially a secret one. The inquest format hadn't been used for years. There would have been an open investigation. But, at that time, Kennedy's people were able to change the rules. They made it a secretive hearing, when originally it was to be an open investigative hearing.

"Everyone at the Kennedy party would have been subpoenaed. Questions would have been asked. That's one of the functions of the grand jury. We weren't allowed to subpoena witnesses. They used the excuse that they had already testified at the inquest. The grand jury, as we found out later, has the right to subpoena anyone it wants. We were told by the D.A. that we weren't allowed to subpoena those people who were directly involved, like Kennedy, Markham, Gargan, all the young ladies that were there at that time. We were just denied that right to question them. This was the most frustrating part of my position as foreman of the grand jury.

"I lost a lot of faith in the justice system. Said it before and I'll say it again. There seems to be two sets of rules: one set for the powerful. And one set for the ordinary working citizen.

"We tried to do the best job possible. I called for the grand jury to reconvene. Dinis did try to exhume the body. Dinis called for the inquest, but unfortunately all records were impounded, and not made available to the public or the grand jury.

"It has been very frustrating, and has continued to bother me all these years. The D.A. told the grand jury that we could not subpoena witnesses that were involved because they already testified at the inquest. Then I went to Judge Paquet to request the inquest documents so the grand jury could look at those documents to see what was in there, but that was denied.

"When inquest documents were released to the public, they found notes from the presiding judge, Judge Boyle, saying a lot of things in many areas that didn't make sense and did not relate to what people said. There were many discrepancies in the testimony, discrepancies that were not scrutinized and questioned. Like the time frame that Kennedy claimed, when he was returning to the ferry that took people from Chappaquiddick to Edgartown. He claims it was around 11:15 p.m. Huck Look, who was a deputy sheriff at the time, adamantly claims he saw an Oldsmobile with Kennedy in it at 12:45 a.m. the next morning, an hour and a half after Kennedy claims he went off the bridge. The judge clearly indicated that there was no way Kennedy made that right turn onto a dirt road by accident. No way you could make that turn without slowing down to almost a complete stop.

"Locals who know the area know you have to stop and make a 90-degree turn to get onto the dirt road. And, when you're on that road, you immediately know you're on a dirt road, not a paved road taking you to the ferry.

"Furthermore, we were not allowed to look at many items. If we were, we might have had enough cause to decide on an indictment and bring the case before a jury, during which time tough questions would have been asked. But the grand jury was shut down by the D.A. and Judge Paquet. At the time it was very frustrating, and remains so to this day. I was 29 at the time. I felt very strongly that people have the right to know what really happened. The grand jury was clearly manipulated.

"Kennedy was deeply affected by the incident. He remained a Senator, but he never fulfilled his dream of becoming President of the United States. I still cannot comprehend how the people of Massachusetts keep voting for him."

Several years ago this co-writer went to Chappaquiddick Island with Leland to view the accident scene. During the visit, Leland expressed more of his views on the incident that has haunted him for some forty years.

"Kennedy's people must have been debating on how they could make him look like a hero," Leland said. "The fact that he claimed to have tried to save her life played nicely to the media. The Kennedy team surely was thinking of how they can make him look like a hero, and save his political career. Here's a Senator aspiring to be president, and we've got a situation where maybe they were having an affair or maybe they were just good friends. But an accident happened. How can we make him look good? The hell with the girl." These were some of the thoughts that haunt Leland to this day.

"That's why I felt and feel so bad. This is about Mary Jo. She's twenty-nine years old. She's gone. That's why I feel so bad. The hell with Ted Kennedy. There's a life gone. A young one at that.

"Ted Kennedy was simply trying to protect his political career. I firmly believe that from day one, things progressed and the key players were saying back off. It was just an accident. It brought me back to that initial meeting in the car, with the Chief of Police and Walter Steele. They were saying it was a simple accident. It happened. Forget it. Just blow it off.

"My thoughts always went to Gwen and Joseph Kopechne. This was their daughter. Their only child. And I felt bad. Then there was Ted Kennedy. He was going to be our next President of the U.S. Those were my thoughts back in those days, and I have since searched my soul many times."

Through the years, Les kept in contact with the Kopechnes. Although they always talked about a personal meeting, the get together never happened. They did, however, continue to talk on the phone.

During their conversations they talked of everything from Gwen and Les's love for ice cream to the way the Kopechnes were treated by the Kennedy team. How they were shielded from the truth. How they were blocked from meeting with their friends, neighbors, and the media after the accident. How the Senator avoided them.

Les describes Gwen as one of the sweetest people he had ever come in contact with. Not a mean bone in her body.

"She was always worried about what might happen to me. She was troubled about my well-being. Gwen constantly expressed her concerns about my safety and welfare.

"As I've stated many times, I still am unable to understand how the sympathy for Senator Kennedy and his loss of a chance at the presidency could overshadow the sad tragedy of a 29-year old young lady who lost her life, which might possibly have been saved."

When the Kopechnes eventually discovered the truth bout what happened that fateful night at Chappaquiddick, it so destroyed Joe that his sorrow contributed to his eventual death from cancer.

"There I was, in a small town, a young 29-year-old pharmacist, entrusted as foreman of the grand jury investigating—or at least trying to—the death of a young woman and the part that this wealthy and influential man played. I agreed to the position because I felt that maybe I could make a difference. You can't do it from the sidelines. You have to be willing to put the next step forward."

As we drove across the island, discussion led to all phases of the case. But if any one thing stands out ... and there are so many discrepancies in the story ... that one thing is the Senator's turning onto the dirt road. Leland described the road as follows:

"As you drive down the paved road on the way to the ferry, you can't miss the fact that the road is banked to the left. You can easily see it, because the road is raised as it goes left. If you take a right it's a ninety-degree turn, a right angle, from the paved road. You would virtually almost have to come to a complete stop. Maybe you could do it at five miles an hour, tops, then turn right and go down this dirt road that takes you to the bridge. No question about it. This was not a wrong turn. This was a conscious decision.

"The Senator claimed he turned on to that road by accident. There is no way you can turn onto that road unless you knowingly want to turn on that road. He claims he went onto it unknowingly. There is no way.

"Now we just went one-tenth of a mile down that dirt road, and we bounced all over. The road is seven-tenths of a mile long to the bridge, I believe, and if I had false teeth they would have fallen out. And we're only doing 10 miles per hour. If I had turned on that road after I had just a couple of drinks, I would have known I was on a dirt road, not a paved one. Also, bear in mind there is a paved road and only one paved road on the island, and if you stay on that paved road it takes you back to the ferry.

"I believe if you're going down that road, Dike Road, and don't know you're on a dirt road, you've got some major problems. This wasn't the first time Kennedy was on Chappaquiddick, and it wasn't the first time he was on the road that day."

On our way back from Chappy to Edgartown, we continued speculating about what had happened that fatal evening. When we talked about Kennedy's return trip, the one in which he supposedly swam across, Les said to me, "How in hell could you or I go to your hotel room, crawl into bed, fall asleep and then get up in the morning, dress immaculately, go out on your little patio, have a cup of coffee, read the newspaper and talk with a couple you sailed with the previous day? How can you explain how someone could come out in the morning as if nothing has happened, and be calm? How can he do that?"

Leland continued expressing his frustrations. "Nobody cared about Mary Jo. All Ted Kennedy cared about was how to save his political career. He comes out like Don Quixote. Hey, as he explained, I tried my best.

"We, the grand jury, let everyone down. According to Judge Paquet, we couldn't subpoena anyone who testified at the inquest. And he denied my request for the inquest transcript of testimony. Paquet stared at me, which I remember vividly. He read from a prepared piece of paper in front of him … denying the grand jury the inquest documents, and saying it would remain impounded until the grand jury was through with its fact-finding. At this point, the jurors wanted to go home. Completely disillusioned. But I wanted to go further. I felt I'd been used, set up. The transcript couldn't be released until the grand jury was dismissed.

"The other members of the jury were supportive of my re-convening the grand jury. We tried to get to the truth. We wanted to see the inquest transcripts. They had heard from me that the D.A. had told me we would find them very interesting, as we would the remarks of the judge … the statements made by Kennedy and made by the girls and those statements and others wouldn't jell. Different stories. Different times. D.A. didn't say we couldn't see it, just that we would find it interesting. He was repeating Paquet's orders.

"The grand jury sure as hell has the right to subpoena witnesses and see the transcripts from the inquest. We are a secretive body. It's what we were there for. Kennedy's power machine changed the ground rules."

CHAPTER 18

WHAT IF?

Let's now investigate what Les Leland and the grand jury might have discovered if they had been allowed to read over the inquest testimony. In Kennedy's testimony he stated, "The first time, I left at approximately 11:15 the evening of July eighteenth, and I left a second time sometime after midnight. By my best judgment, it would be approximately 12:15 for the second time. On the second occasion I never left the cottage itself; I left the immediate vicinity of the cottage, which was probably fifteen or twenty feet outside the front door."

He continued, "Sometime after I left the second time, I returned to Edgartown. I did not return immediately to Edgartown."

Earlier, when asked how long he stayed on Chappaquiddick, he responded: "Well, to my best knowledge, I would say 1:30 in the morning on July nineteenth."

When asked about the car, Kennedy originally stated that the window on the driver's side was open. Later in his testimony, he said, "I can remember reaching what I thought was down, which was really up, to where I thought the window was, and feeling along the side to see if the window was open, and the window was closed."

A few moments later, when describing his efforts to get both Mary Jo and himself out of the car, he was asked if the window was closed at that time. He responded, "The window was open." When asked if he was referring to the driver's side, he said, "That's correct."

During his testimony, the Judge asked Kennedy if he ever realized, while driving on an unpaved dirt road at twenty miles per hour, that he was on the wrong road. The Senator stated, "No."

In his written statement, you will also recall that Kennedy concluded by saying, "When I fully realized what had happened this morning, I immediately contacted the police." This, of course, was another bit of Kennedy fiction. He previously said he reported the accident some time before 10 a.m. This clearly was not immediate. Moreover, phone records presented at the inquest show that he made a call at 10:57 a.m. on July 19 that lasted for twenty-three minutes and fifty-four seconds.

Kennedy stated that he left for the party from the Shiretown Inn and arrived on Chappaquiddick around 7:30 p.m. Yet Charles Tretter testified that Mr. Kennedy was at the party house at about 6:30 p.m. Another discrepancy.

Kennedy said he asked LaRosa to get Gargan, then asked Gargan to get Markham. LaRosa stated that Kennedy asked him to get Gargan and Markham at the same time. Still another discrepancy.

In Mr. Tretter's testimony, he stated that the "Senator had called he and Mr. Markham out of the cottage, had told them what had happened, and asked to be driven to the Edgartown Ferry, and Mr. Gargan said the Senator was distraught, that neither one of them talked to him. He just kept saying, get me to Edgartown, get me to Edgartown. So Mr. Gargan was saying that we drove to Edgartown; the Senator dove off of the slip and swam across, and that they went into the water after him." Another twist to the story.

Joe Gargan testified that he arrived at the cottage on Chappaquiddick at about 7:00 p.m., and that he left immediately to go back to the ferry landing to pick up some people. He was asked if he returned to the house, and he replied, "I did." He was then questioned about how many trips he took from the cottage to the ferry landing, and he said only one. He stated he arrived back at the house close to 8:30 p.m. Now, why would it take one and one half hours to go from the house to the ferry landing and back? This is typically a 15-or-20-minute trip.

When asked approximately what time in the morning he told some of the guests about the accident, Gargan said that it was about 9:00 a.m. The questions went on:

Q: Who did you tell?

A: I told the girls.

Q: At the cottage?

A: That is correct, and Jack Crimmins.

Q: This is nine o'clock at the Chappaquiddick cottage?

A: That is correct.

Q: You told everyone there?

A: Not everybody was there, but I mean everybody that was at the cottage, yes.

Q: Who left?

A: Cricket Keough and Suzie Tannenbaum left.

Q: Who was still there?

A: Well, to the best of my recollection, Your Honor, it would be Jack Crimmins, Ray LaRosa and the five girls.

Q: And you told them all at that time what had happened?

A: Yes.

In reviewing this testimony, consider:

1) if Cricket and Suzie left, there would not have been five girls remaining;

2) only Jack Crimmins was originally mentioned, then LaRosa was added;

3) the story told by others was that they were only told that Mary Jo was missing, not what had actually happened.

Later in his testimony, Gargan said he was not at the cottage until 9:00 a.m., but that he left the cottage and took the ferry across to Edgartown around 8:00. He said he went with Tretter, Tannenbaum, Keough, and Markham. So, which of these statements in his sworn testimony do you believe?

During all the questioning, in spite of reports to the contrary, all the partygoers stated that they had one or two drinks at the most. During the questioning of Paul Markham, the following took place:

Q: Do you recall whether or not Mr. Kennedy had anything to drink?

A: Yes.

Q: Could you tell the court what?

A: A rum and Coke, at this point.

Q: He had a rum and Coke at this point?

A: Yes.

Q: How did you know he did?

A: Because he said to Jack Crimmins, "Who has been drinking all the rum, there is hardly any rum left."

John B. Crimmins testified that he had bought liquor in Boston and brought it to the cottage. He had purchased three half-gallons of vodka, four fifths of scotch, two bottles of rum, and a couple of cases of beer, certainly a sufficient supply for twelve guests.

Christopher F. "Huck" Look was an oil dealer and part-time deputy sheriff. The evening of the eighteenth he was at the Edgartown Yacht Club. He stated that he left the Yacht Club around 12:25 a.m., and upon leaving the Yacht Club, "I went out on the launch which belongs to the Edgartown Yacht Club, which is the practice, and they took me over to Chappaquiddick and I proceeded to my home."

The examination of "Huck" Look went on:

Q: You say you got into your automobile. Then what did you do?

A: I proceeded up towards my home.

Q: How do you get to your home?

A: You go up the macadamized road.

Q: Which is known as?

A: I think it is Chappaquiddick Road or Main Street. I really don't know what the true name of the road is, sir.

Q: Where did you go from Chappaquiddick Road? Does it go onto Schoolhouse Road?

A: Yes.

Q: Is that a continuation of the road?

A: Yes, of the macadamized part of the road.

Q: Are you familiar with what is known as Dike Road?

A: Yes, sir.

Q: Now, would you tell us what time approximately you were at Chappaquiddick Road, at this juncture with Schoolhouse Road and Dike Road?

A: Well, I have driven the road many times, and I would say it would take me until approximately twenty minutes of 1:00 to quarter of 1:00 to reach the point, the corner and Dike Road.

Q: So you say approximately 12:40 to 12:45 you were on that juncture?

A: Yes, sir, approximately.

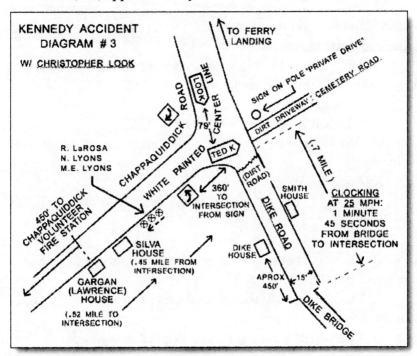

Courtesy Ytedk.com

Q: Did you see anyone or anything?

A: As I approached it, I saw a car coming from the right-hand side.

Q: Would that be Schoolhouse Road?

A: Yes, sir.

Q: Did you have occasion to notice anything about it?

A: You mean make?

Q: Make or size?

A: I noticed it was a dark car that passed in front of me.

Q: Where did it go when it passed in front of you?

A: It went into a little dirt road, maybe ten feet off the road that is commonly known, I believe, as Cemetery Road, and it stopped, and as it stopped I proceeded around the corner and looked into the mirror of my car and noticed the car started to back up. Usually, on Chappaquiddick, people get lost quite often, and I stopped in case they wanted to ask me which direction is the ferry, or this way, or that house, and I stopped when they started to back up towards me, and got out of my car and walked back towards the car.

Q: How far had you traveled up Schoolhouse Road when you observed this car backing out of what you described as Cemetery Road or Lane?

A: I think it is around two and a half miles.

Q: How far were you from the intersection when you stopped?

A: Around 25 feet.

Q: All right. You stopped your car when you saw the lights back up?

A: Right.

Q: Do you know how far this automobile which you saw entered into Cemetery Lane?

A: I would say that the back wheels just got off the macadamized road.

Q: And you saw the lights, you stopped and you got out?

A: Yes, sir.

Q: How far away were you from this car when you stopped your car, and from the point where you saw its back wheels were just off the macadam road?

A: Somewhere around 50 or 60 feet.

Q: Tell us exactly what you did. You stopped your car and you got out?

A: I didn't stop it at first. I almost came to a stop and I saw the lights coming from my right-hand side, which would be in the direction of the fire station, coming towards me, and I practically came to a complete stop because the automobiles, when they make that large corner, usually cut it very close, and I was afraid I might run into him, and the car passed directly in front of me about 35 feet away from my car, my headlights were on this car, and right across and then stopped. I continued around the corner and stopped, and I noticed the car lights were backing up, and I said to myself, "Well, they probably want some information," so I stopped my car and got out and started to walk back to them on Cemetery Road. I got about 25 or 30 feet when the car was backing up and backed towards the ferry landing on the macadamized road, and then it drove down the Dike Road.

Q: Now, at your closest point to this car how far were you from it, at its closest point?

A: Twenty-five or thirty feet.

Q: Are there any lights at that intersection?

A: No, sir.

Q: Were there any lights either by your motor vehicle or that motor vehicle at that time? Were they on?

A: Yes.

Q: Including its rear lights?

A: Yes, sir.

Q: And what did you observe about the car at that time, if anything?

A: That it was a dark car and that it was a Massachusetts registration.

Q: What did you notice, if anything, about the registration?

A: That it began with an L and it had a seven at the beginning and one at the end.

Q: Did you observe anything about its occupants?

A: When the automobile passed in front of me, and also when I was walking towards it, there appeared to be a man driving and a woman in the front right-hand side, and also either another person or an object of clothing, a handbag or something, sitting on the back. It looked to me like an object of some kind. I couldn't say what it would be.

Later on in the questioning, Look said it was a moonlit night and that he saw the car go down the road, though he couldn't tell how far the car traveled. "There was a lot of dust, and all I could see was just the lights going on down the road."

The deputy sheriff then told about an encounter with some people walking down the road. "As I approached them, it would be a tall girl, and a little shorter one, and a fairly short man."

When asked about these people walking, Huck Look said he stopped his car and asked if they would like a lift.

"The tall one said, 'Shove off, buddy, or shove off, mister, we are not pickups,' or something to that effect. When I was about to get out of the car, the man said, 'No thank you, sir. We are only going to this place over here.' And he pointed in the direction of the Lawrence cottage."

This statement by Huck Look is in concert with Ray LaRosa's testimony when he recalled the same incident. LaRosa, who was walking with the Lyons sisters, also remembers another car passing them, but not stopping, before the incident with Look.

John Farrar, captain of the Edgartown Fire Department Search and Rescue Division (Scuba Search and Rescue Division), recovered Mary Jo's body. A scuba diver for more than eighteen years, he carefully described the procedures he undertook in getting Mary Jo's body out of the car. After removing the body, he returned to the wreckage and removed the purse from the headliner inside the car. That's probably the object that "Huck" Look saw in the right rear of the automobile.

During the questioning, Farrar told about the condition of the doors and windows of the car: "I noted that the two windows on the right-hand front door and rear door were blown out with the glass smashed, and most of the glass shattered and spread throughout the car as if from impact. The left-hand side window, the driver's window, was rolled down to within an inch of the bottom. The driver's door was locked. The snap button was pressed down. The only window intact was the left rear window.

"The windshield was ostensibly smashed; however, the safety rim holding the window was virtually intact. In other words, it was not blown out as were the two right windows."

During Chief Dominick J. Arena's testimony, he related how he would try to locate Senator Kennedy when he found out it was the Senator's car.

"John Ahlbum, the owner of the Depot Corner Service Station, had arrived at the scene, and I was walking by him as I got up on the bridge, and I made a remark that this was Senator Kennedy's car, and he said to me, 'I just saw him down by the ferry landing,' so at this time I proceeded right to Mrs. Malm's house and I called with the intent of advising my office, my desk officer, to send someone down to the ferry landing to see if they could find Senator Kennedy."

When asked about what time this all occurred, Arena continued:

"Now, time once again I would have to say it would have been after nine o'clock, but I don't really know how much time elapsed. At any rate, when I called her (the desk officer, Mrs. Albocter) she said 'He is here.' This is Mrs. Albocter. She meant the Senator, and he wanted to talk to me, so he got on the phone and I said words to the effect that 'I am sorry, I have some bad news, your car was in an accident over here and the young lady is dead.' He said, 'I know.'

"I said, 'Can you tell me was there anybody in the car?'
"He said, 'Yes.'
"I said, 'Are they in the water.'
"He said, 'No.'
"I said, 'Can I talk to you?'
"He said, 'Yes.'
"I said, 'Would you like to talk to me?'
"He said, 'I prefer for you to come over here.'"

Paul Markham and the Senator were in the chief's office when Arena arrived. The Senator was on the phone, but hung up when Arena walked into the office. Kennedy shook the chief's hand, and Arena said something about being sorry about what had happened. Then Kennedy told the chief that he was the driver.

Kennedy asked Arena, "What would you like for me to do, we must do what is right or we will both be criticized for it." Chief Arena then told the Senator he must have a statement of what happened.

During his questioning, the chief was asked about "Huck" Look, and whether or not they had a conversation about the car that was removed from the water.

"He didn't. At the time he said something about how he had seen some people at the intersection the night before. Later on, I found out that he had talked to Officer Brougier, and said that he had thought he had seen the same car at the intersection the night before, and as a result of this I took a statement from Mr. Look concerning that car," Arena testified.

During testimony given by Maryellen Lyons, she related the behavior of everyone when Gargan and Markham returned to the cottage. She described their statements as "confusing." She said they had been told that Mary Jo was back at Katama Shores. She thought it was Mr. Gargan who had told them.

Q: Did anyone ask where the Senator's car was?

Maryellen: Well, Mary Jo had taken the car on the last ferry.

Q: Mary Jo had taken the car on the last ferry, and who told you that; was it Mr. Gargan?

Maryellen: Yes, as I remember, it was Mr. Gargan.

Q: Told you that Mary Jo had taken the Senator's car and gone back to Katama and that the Senator had swam across the channel. I don't want to be repetitive. Now, what else happened? Were there any further questions about these particular events?

Maryellen: Not really.

Q: Did you find them unusual?

Maryellen: Not at the time; no, I didn't.

CHAPTER 19

JUDGE BOYLE'S SUMMARY

In his summation after the inquest, Judge Boyle concluded in writing with the following facts:

a. Kennedy was the host, and was mainly responsible for, the assembly of the group at Edgartown.

b. Kennedy was rooming at Shiretown with Gargan, his cousin and close friend for many years.

c. Kennedy had employed Crimmins as chauffeur for nine years, and rarely drove himself. Crimmins drove Kennedy on all other occasions herein set forth, and was available at the time of the fatal trip.

d. Kennedy told only Crimmins that he was leaving for Shiretown, and requested the car key.

e. The young women were close friends, were on Martha's Vineyard for a common purpose as a cohesive group, and staying together at Katama Shores.

f. Kopechne roomed with Newburgh, the latter having in her possession the key to their room.

g. Kopechne told no one, other than Kennedy, that she was leaving for Katama Shores, and did not ask Newburgh for the room key.

h. Kopechne left her pocketbook at the cottage when she drove off with Kennedy.

i. It was known that the ferry ceased operation about midnight, and special arrangements must be made for a later trip. No such arrangements were made.

j. Ten of the persons at the cookout did not intend to remain at the cottage overnight.

k. Only the Oldsmobile and the Valiant were available for transportation of those ten, the Valiant being the smaller car.

l. LaRosa's Mercury was parked at Shiretown, and was available for use.

I infer a reasonable and probable explanation of the totality of the above facts is that Kennedy and Kopechne did not intend to return to Edgartown at that time; that Kennedy did not intend to drive to the ferry slip, and his turn onto Dike Road was intentional. Having reached this conclusion, the question then arises as to whether there was anything criminal in his operation of the motor vehicle.

From two personal views which corroborate the engineer's statement, and other evidence, I am fully convinced that Dike Bridge constitutes a traffic hazard, particularly so at night, and must be approached with extreme caution. A speed of even twenty miles per hour, as Kennedy testified to, operating a car as large as this Oldsmobile, would at least be negligent and, possibly, reckless. If Kennedy knew of this hazard, his operation of the vehicle constituted criminal conduct.

Earlier on July 18, he had been driven over Chappaquiddick Road three times, and over Dike Road and Dike Bridge twice. Kopechne had been driven over Chappaquiddick Road five times, and over Dike Road and Dike Bridge twice.

I believe it probable that Kennedy knew of the hazard that lay ahead of him on Dike Road, but that, for some reason not apparent from the testimony, he failed to exercise due care as he approached the bridge.

I, therefore, find there is probable cause to believe that Edward M. Kennedy operated his motor vehicle negligently on a way or in a place to which the public have a right of access, and that such operation appears to have contributed to the death of Mary Jo Kopechne.

Earlier in his summation, Judge Boyle stated that in concert with the Massachusetts Supreme Court decision concerning the conduct of an inquest, "The inquest serves as an aid in the achievement of justice by obtaining information as to whether a crime has been committed." He cited a case from 1945 in which the court said, "It is designed merely to ascertain facts for the purpose of subsequent prosecution" and "the investigating judge may himself issue process against a person whose probable guilt is disclosed."

He continued by rejecting that the cardinal principle of "proof beyond a reasonable doubt" applied in criminal trials, but used as a standard the principle of "probable guilt."

In this summation, Boyle quoted from a particular case, "A presumption of fact is an inference which a reasonable man would draw from certain facts which have been proven." He goes on from the evidence section, which states, "A presumption of fact or an inference is nothing more than a probable or natural explanation of facts ... and arises from the commonly accepted experiences of mankind and the inferences which reasonable men would draw from experiences."

Based on his findings and conclusions, why was the Senator slapped on the hands with a "leaving the scene of an accident" verdict, and not something more severe, as indicated by Judge Boyle's findings and conclusion?

Joe and Gwen Kopechne with Mary Jo, when she was 12.

CHAPTER 20

LELAND'S REACTION

When Leland was finally able to read the transcript of the inquest, he was even more incensed at what had taken place. "As I look back at it, I still find it hard to believe all the maneuvering that went on to ensure the innocence and lack of prosecution that should have been dealt to Ted Kennedy ... because he was who he was.

"You know we've lived with, and I say 'we' meaning the grand jury, have suffered with the innuendo that there was a cover-up or a whitewash, that we were paid off. To live with that accusation and not be able to speak to the issue really haunts me.

"I found out later that the grand jury indeed had the right to subpoena any witnesses; we had the right to subpoena any witnesses that we wanted to—it's one of the basic functions of the grand jury. The second thing is that, even though the judge denied us the inquest transcript, the district attorney could have, on our behalf, appealed to the superior court, and the chances are a thousand to one that the inquest transcript would have been released to the grand jury because the grand jury is a secretive body, and the only reason the inquest was impounded to begin with was so it wasn't made available to the press and the public. Judge Boyle could have called the grand jury into session easily, based on his written observations."

After the accident, Leland said he had a lot of conversations with the district attorney. "The reporters were asking me, what we were going to do, when are you going to start the investigation?

"I went to the district attorney. When I look back on this now, his approach is very clear to me. He said, 'Well, you have the right to investigate this accident.' I said, 'Why don't you investigate, you're the district attorney—you are the one who is skilled and you're paid to do that job, that's your profession.' And he sort of ignored that and kept pushing for me to do it.

"I then called the state attorney general and asked the same questions of him. I got a different answer from him. He said that the district attorney would be the proper one to investigate—but it was very clear to me that Dinis did not want to get involved. I didn't understand why at the time, but I certainly do now. He was a Democrat, up for re-election … he probably also had some ties with the Kennedys … so he was in a situation where, if he had gotten the grand jury to call for the investigation, he could then say to his fellow Democrats, 'Look, I'm doing a job that I have to because I am the district attorney, the grand jury is the one that called for the investigation.' Whereas if he had initiated it, it wouldn't sit so well with the political machinery. So, I went through that ordeal. I had that conversation with Dinis more than once, because he was still sort of pushing for me to do it. Later, the district attorney told me he would keep me informed of what was going on in his investigation. At that point, he said, he didn't need to bring the grand jury into the situation."

Leland related that the jury members were frustrated and disgusted. "We were road-blocked in every way. The judge and district attorney rendered us useless. We couldn't do the job we were selected to do." Then Leland recalled his conversation with Jack Melemey who described a runaway grand jury. A runaway grand jury is one in which the grand jurors have taken control of the investigation and are ignoring the prosecutor's efforts to rein them in. In the nineteenth century, many American grand juries were crotchety and independent, and did what they wanted. Later in the twentieth century, grand juries had pretty much come under the control of prosecutors.

A runaway grand jury is an exception to this rule—the grand jurors ignore the prosecutor(s) and start making their own decisions. Runaway grand juries were not uncommon in the early twentieth century. The best known of these runaway grand juries is probably the New York grand jury in the 1930s that barred prosecutors from coming into the grand jury room, and took off on its own investigation of corruption in New York city government. This grand jury eventually cooperated with Thomas E. Dewey, whom jurors apparently decided they could trust, and returned many indictments against a variety of defendants, including some well-known members of the New York Mafia. Since modern grand jurors tend to be ignorant of their ability to act independently of a prosecutor's wishes, runaway grand juries have pretty much become a thing of the past.

There have, however, been a few exceptions. Recently, for example, a California state grand jury indicted all the top county officials, and nearly closed down county government. And, a Texas state grand jury began investigating a mayoral candidate, and seems to have ruined his reputation sufficiently to cause him to lose the election, even though he was never charged with any crimes.

As Leland said, "If we had only known what we could do, things would have been completely different. The old saying 'ignorance is bliss' is certainly not applicable in what we were forced to live with."

In talking about the inquest, Leland was shocked, after reading the transcript, that the case was basically dropped. "There are so many discrepancies in the testimony that it is really hard to tell truth from fiction. Let's just take a look at a few of them. Kennedy stated that he reported the accident to the police the next morning before 10 a.m. Yet the phone company witness stated that Kennedy made a call at 10:57 a.m. that lasted for 23 minutes and 54 seconds. Perhaps that has nothing to do with the accident, but why not tell the truth?

"Charley Tretter's story of how he learned of the accident and what he was told differs from the story told by Kennedy, Markham and Gargan. The timing of many of the occurrences differs from witness to witness. Testimony from all the witnesses agreed that there was very limited drinking by all of the party guests, but look at the amount of liquor that was purchased and the number of empty bottles found after everyone departed the cottage. On top of that, Mary Jo supposedly was said to have had a blood alcohol level of .09 percent, the equivalent of 3.75 to 5 ounces of 80- to 90-proof liquor within an hour of death, or up to five drinks. Very unusual for a slight girl who normally didn't drink, and reportedly only had a drink or so that night.

"Or how about one of the young ladies' testimony that Gargan had told her that Mary Jo had taken Kennedy's car on the last ferry, but that Kennedy had swam across the channel? Then there's LaRosa's testimony about the two cars that were seen on the road at two different times. Obviously, his testimony coincides with that of Huck Look. The description of what happened with his car is exactly the same as the testimony of the cottage's guests. Then, there's the question of why Mary Jo left without her purse.

"Why didn't Kennedy report the accident for ten or more hours? Could it have been that he was legally intoxicated and needed that time to sober up so that blood tests would show nothing unusual? Kennedy claimed he had a little beer in the afternoon and two drinks in the evening. Yet, in Leo Damore's book *Senatorial Privilege*, he states that Stan Moore, who sent his boat to pick up Kennedy for a victory party in the afternoon, said that he and Kennedy had three drinks each. He remembered because they were both drinking rum and Coke. The book also covers the drinking of Paul Markham at the party, who was drinking heavily because of an injured leg, and Jack Crimmins, who was arguing with Kennedy because Kennedy had quite a few. According to the book, Gargan observed 'everybody's a little bombed except for Ray LaRosa.'

"Then there's also discrepancies in the stories as to whether Kennedy came back and asked for Gargan and later for Markham, or whether he asked for both of them at the same time. And what about the time difference in Kennedy's and Gargan's testimony?

Based on the statements, Gargan should have returned to the cottage somewhere in the vicinity of 1 a.m., but he testified that he returned at 2:15 a.m.

"Perhaps these issues may not be meaningful in themselves, but when you add them all up you wonder what really happened, what the actual story was, why was everyone so protective of Kennedy, yet cared so little about justice for Mary Jo.

"How about Judge Boyle's findings and opinion? Why weren't charges brought, or at least his opinions provided to the grand jury? When you consider all the privileges provided the Senator and the protection he received, you certainly know that not everyone is treated equally. It's almost humorous if it wasn't such a miscarriage of justice, but on the cover of a book by Richard L. and Thomas L. Tedrow, entitled *Death at Chappaquiddick*, Senator Kennedy is quoted, 'Do we operate under a system of equal justice under the law? Or is there one system for the average citizen and another for the high and mighty?' Now, is that chutzpah? I'll never understand how and why the people of Massachusetts continue to vote for him."

Les Leland at an interview session.

Chapter 21

More Versions of What Happened

John Farrar, captain of the Edgartown fire department's Search and Rescue division, had his own version of what happened during the accident. He had been down at the accident scene, and drew his own conclusions that were not favorable to Kennedy. Farrar believed the car was traveling faster than Kennedy had testified, about 30 miles per hour. He stated the car would have hit the water at about a 45-degree angle. After impact, and with the car upside down, he believed that Mary Jo was in a "conscious position" in the back seat, and was able to breathe her own air. "The oxygen content was lowering from 21 percent, and she used it up and replaced it with carbon dioxide. As the CO_2 builds up, you breathe heavier and heavier; the emotional trauma is extensive. Try putting a paper bag over your head and breathing. You can feel the anxiety coming over you. Then try to imagine that bag being held over your head by a 300-pound wrestler, and think of having to struggle to get out of that situation, knowing you might be breathing your last breath. It's a very, very scary situation. The anxiety that sets in is just unbelievable."

Nobody can say for certain, but Farrar believed that "she could have lived for a good while after the car went off the bridge. She was alive, easily an hour."

At a special autopsy hearing on October 20, 1969, Farrar was called as a witness. Dinis examined Farrar and completely avoided any questions that would enable him to expound upon his theory. Farrar was obviously very disappointed that he did not have the opportunity to explain his theory and provide credence to the length of time Mary Jo could have been alive in the car . . . and, most importantly, possibly saved.

Prior to the accident, a Boston newspaper reported that a New Hampshire woman had survived five hours in a submerged automobile. Doctors attributed this miracle to an air bubble trapped inside the car. This incident added credence to Farrar's theory.

"Huck" Look also testified at the hearing, and his statements at that time did not vary from his testimony at the inquest two months later. He saw this large black car sometime around 12:45 a.m. He remembered part of the license plate, and that he could see the numbers because there were back-up lights, tail lights and license plate lights. He remembered that the driver appeared confused, and that he drove away hurriedly at about 25 to 30 miles per hour.

Further testimony from a battery of experts all agreed that the determination of death could not be finalized without an autopsy. Dr. Mills' explanation was too simplified to be meaningful; much of what he said and determined could easily be dismissed as pedestrian analytics.

Les Leland stated that if you believe Markham and Gargan returned to the cottage somewhere around 2:15 a.m., then you can easily accept the testimony of "Huck" Look. If you review it, Kennedy said he returned to the cottage at 12:15 a.m. The three of them immediately drove to Dike Bridge. In testifying, Markham and Gargan said they spent about 45 minutes going down after Mary Jo. That would bring it to about 1:05 a.m. Then they drove the Senator to the ferry landing.

If this is true, what did they do until 2:15 that morning? Remember, too, that LaRosa and the girls saw Look's car, and the timing coincides perfectly with his testimony. In addition, Leland asks why there weren't questions when Tretter stated that he and Rosemary "Cricket" Keough had taken a walk sometime after 11:30 p.m. If Kennedy had returned at 12:15 a.m. he would have run into the two of them. Yet this testimony and timing was never questioned.

Leland also unveiled the story of a waitress and her assistant manager, who had left their jobs at the Harborside Hotel and went to the lighthouse beach on Edgartown at about 12:30 a.m. The waitress told investigators that they saw a large American automobile speeding on the road leading to the ferry landing. She said the car stopped and turned off its lights. It seemed strange, she said, because the ferry had already stopped running. Now, if Kennedy had driven the car off the bridge at about 11:20 p.m., whose car was it that these two people saw? Just a coincidence? Or another fact completely ignored by the police and the prosecution?

Dr. John McHugh, a lab director, examined the car after it was taken out of Poucha Pond. Leland pointed out that what he said was also interesting. The doctor said that the windshield had "caved in like a wave of water hit it from the front," indicating that the car had not merely toppled off Dike Bridge, but had been traveling at considerable speed. What is particularly interesting, Leland noted, was that the driver's side window is 16 inches by 28 inches. How, then, could a 200-pound man with a back brace, pinned upside down beneath the steering wheel, get out?

According to the doctor's theory, since he didn't believe that Kennedy had the dexterity of a contortionist, the door might possibly have sprung open at impact and was closed again by the current. However, if this did happen, how did this door become locked as Farrar testified?

In an article written by Jim Kouri for *Police Times*, the author interviewed NYPD Detective Tony Ulasewicz.

The author asked: One important assignment you received was to investigate the death of Mary Jo Kopechne that resulted from her being in a car with Senator Ted Kennedy at Chappaquiddick. You've gone on the record saying that the subsequent investigation into the incident—whereby Kennedy's automobile ended up submerged in a pond, killing Mary Jo—was a cover-up from the very beginning. What leads you to believe that theory?

Tony: Well, the evidence is extensive. For instance, the medical examiner, Dr. Donald Mills, never performed an autopsy. In fact, he pronounced Mary Jo's death as being "death by drowning" with merely a simple visual exam. My experience as a homicide detective told me that Kopechne didn't drown. I saw white foam around her mouth, which indicates she died due to lack of oxygen. In other words, there must have been an air pocket in the submerged vehicle, and she was able to live perhaps two or three hours after the car hit the water. She suffocated due to lack of oxygen. She didn't drown. Another theory—far more shocking if true—is that Mary Jo was suffocated prior to the car plunging into the pond.

Author: You also say many of Kennedy's staff were all over the island. What were they doing?

Tony: They were covering up. When Kennedy escaped from the submerged vehicle, the first thing he did was telephone staff members rather than call the cops or an ambulance. I was able to get the phone records. His claims of being disoriented as a result of an auto accident seem disingenuous when you consider he had the orientation to remember and dial many phone numbers to get the cover-up mobilized. For instance, some man showed up at the Edgartown police station, where the investigation was being conducted, and asked for a pocketbook that was discovered inside Kennedy's car. The police desk officer turned it over to the man without making a blotter (logbook) entry or even IDing the guy. The officer admitted he just turned it over, no questions asked.

Also, a Kennedy staffer took custody of Mary Jo's remains, saying he was responsible for shipping the body back to her hometown in Pennsylvania. No autopsy. Just a preliminary exam, and out the door goes Mary Jo.

Author: How did Kennedy avoid news media scrutiny?

Tony: Well, I decided that the news media were being fed misinformation by the Kennedy spin-doctors. Whoever they were, they had a casual attitude towards the facts. For instance, the news media told the public that Kennedy made a wrong turn because he was unfamiliar with Chappaquiddick. Well, first, I examined the crime or accident scene myself, and if Kennedy turned the way he said he did, he would have ended either in the bushes or slamming into a telephone pole. Kennedy also said in his statement that he'd never been in that particular area before, which was why he was unfamiliar with the landscape.

I interviewed a number of residents on the island who said they routinely saw all the Kennedy brothers and relatives on the island, including Ted.

The cover-up included people being rushed off the island—people who partied with Kennedy. They were never questioned by the small-town police officers, who were in over their heads. These partygoers, instead, were "debriefed" by Kennedy staffers.

Author: Were the cops bought off?

Tony: I don't think so. These small-town cops had no experience investigating homicides or big cases. They were also dealing with some very powerful people. The Edgartown cops just didn't have any reason to stick their necks out.

In reading Leo Damore's book, Leland remembers that Paul Markham revealed "what really happened" to Edward Harrington. "Paul told me Joe Gargan was the force that kept insisting the accident be reported. Teddy Kennedy didn't want to do it. He wasn't in shock, he was evaluating the situation, looking for a way out from under the thing. Ted couldn't accept the fact he was driving the car. He couldn't deal with it."

Also interesting was the account of the end of the Kennedy-Gargan relationship. Under pressure from various groups, Kennedy accused his close friend, cousin and confidant of "sitting on your ass all winter doing nothing."

Gargan had been spending years putting his life back together and joining Alcoholics Anonymous. He exploded, reportedly saying, "I've given you thirty years of my life and what do I have to show for it? I'm a fool in the eyes of my own children because of Chappaquiddick. And that's your problem, not mine." Leland said he knew Gargan would want the real story told one day. Imagine, Leland said, what a good friend Ted Kennedy was . . . loyal to the end.

Leland also recalls the theory expounded by Jack Anderson, a syndicated columnist, who interviewed numerous Kennedy "intimates." His column stated that Kennedy had deliberately turned off because he was going to take Miss Kopechne swimming at East Beach. He had drunk a lot that night, but his friends say he wasn't drunk. Driving too fast, Kennedy's car skidded off the bridge. When it sank, he was able to escape. He made several attempts to save the girl, but was unsuccessful. He gave up and swam to the shore to rest.

While on the shore resting, he thought of all the ways he could save, and I'll never forget this term, "his presidential dream." At the time, he also conjured up the scheme to ask his cousin to take the rap for him. Gargan agreed to say he was driving, and went back to the scene to familiarize himself with the area. Then Gargan and Markham rustled up a boat and rowed the Senator to the other side, where he snuck into the Shiretown Inn. Anderson stated that Kennedy even went down to talk to a room clerk, so that everyone would know he was there. The next morning Kennedy, with his confidants, went over to Chappaquiddick to look at the scene, but found that the car had already been discovered. While Leland admits that the story may not be factual, he also states that you can't really dispute it because no one, other than the Senator, really knows what happened.

CHAPTER 22

NOW WHAT?

Some forty years later, Les Leland, still unsatisfied with all the happenings of this tragic case, stated: "I know that there was a cover-up going on. As I look back, I realize a lot of manipulation went on."

Not only did Leland receive death threats; he discovered that John Farrar reportedly also got death threats. Farrar was ordered to keep quiet about his findings. He had told Leland and others that the Kennedy team did a professional job in doing everything they could to avoid implicating the Senator. Farrar was not allowed to testify as to his findings. He could only answer questions as they were asked, and could not relate his investigative information that allowed Mary Jo could have lived up to two hours after the car tumbled into the pond. Farrar had said that the situation was very carefully guarded as to what questions could be asked and what questions would be answered. Anyone who was going to give answers contrary to the Kennedy story was not allowed to testify on those specific issues.

Farrar was told to "keep quiet or there could be trouble." Some two years after the Chappaquiddick incident, a gun-wielding assailant was said to have assaulted Farrar in a hotel room after he was interviewed about the accident and his beliefs on a Boston radio station.

Leland said, "We, the grand jury, wanted to do what was right. All of us felt disillusioned with the justice system when we were illegally told what we couldn't do ... couldn't call witnesses who testified at the inquest. That's illegal. Couldn't read the transcript of the inquest. That's illegal. We just didn't know. We were manipulated, I guess, because of our stupidity and lack of knowledge at the time. Yet the district attorney and the judge misled us. All they were concerned about was protecting Kennedy's career and political future. It was like, the hell with the fact that this young lady lost her life.

"We were sworn to secrecy for life. Imagine that! And we believed it until we found out that, too, was illegal. But at the time, I could just see being out there talking to the press or the public, and being dragged back into court for speaking the truth. I felt strongly that the public had a right to know. Yet we were blocked from doing our job.

"Why couldn't Kennedy just tell the truth? In his initial statement to the police, he said he walked back to the cottage and 'asked for someone' to take him to Edgartown. In his televised speech he made no mention of asking for someone to take him to Edgartown, but instead said he asked Gargan and Markham to return to the bridge.

"He says he was driving at seven or eight miles an hour on a paved road. Then turned right onto Dike Road and was driving approximately twenty miles per hour. That doesn't even make sense. Then he said he didn't know he was on a dirt road immediately. That's absolutely impossible.

"There were numerous telephone calls made; a complete list was supplied to the court. The first was made Friday at 10:08 a.m., but the Senator supposedly did not arrive until after 1:00 p.m. Another at 12:30 p.m. and still another at 6:39 p.m. One call on Saturday morning was at 10:57 a.m., an hour or so after he said he reported the accident to the police. Kennedy made another call from Chappaquiddick at 9:30 a.m., and several from the police station. He called the Kopechnes at about 10 a.m., told them of the accident, but never even mentioned that he was involved. One newspaper reported that the Senator made seventeen calls during the hours he supposedly was in shock.

"Even after the inquest and the judge's conclusion that there was probable cause to believe that Kennedy's negligent driving had 'contributed to the death of Mary Jo Kopechne,' District Attorney Dinis still refused to seek the manslaughter indictment.

"What upset all of us jurors was the underlying sentiment that perhaps we were paid off. That bothered all of us. And it still does. Of course, this wasn't the only thing. Just the way we were manipulated was something none of us will ever get over. Could it happen today? I certainly hope not.

"Here is a man who was seeking the highest political office in the country. The man who holds that position must have integrity and the trust of the people. But Ted Kennedy was not totally honest about the events on Chappaquiddick. Also, the job of president of the United States requires the ability to stand up under pressure. Senator Kennedy was not able to do that at Chappaquiddick.

"Was there justice? You've got to be kidding. The whole thing stinks. Massachusetts got a black eye that day that still remains. The people of the state know it. There are two sets of laws—one for the Kennedys, the powerful and elitists—and one for everyone else.

"There is no question in my mind that a big political machine was operating. I have never been so disappointed in the workings of democracy as when I was on that grand jury, watching all kinds of legal and illegal maneuvering taking place. I really felt, and still feel, sick inside. Every avenue to get at the facts was blocked.

"I have never voted for Kennedy since that incident. Whenever he ran I would vote for his opponent, whoever it might be.

"When informed of the Kopechne's intention to sue, Senator Kennedy agreed to pay $90,923, the difference between the $50,000 the insurance company agreed to and the amount of accident insurance on the Senator's car.

"And Huck Look steadfastly backed his story. He simply stated to the end whenever he was questioned, 'It just becomes, as I told everybody, a thing of credibility. If you want to believe him, fine. If you want to believe me, I've got nothing to gain in any way, shape, or form.'

"With all of the discrepancies, with all of the illegal maneuvering, with all of the public relations efforts put on by the Kennedy team, with all of the poor investigating and prosecuting, the thing that stands out to me the most is how a man can be in an accident like this, with a woman dead in his car, and he goes back to his hotel, spends the rest of the night sleeping, wakes up the next morning, dresses and meets with people as if nothing had happened. Perhaps a hardened criminal might be able to compose himself, but I just can't understand a normal person behaving like that."

Chapter 23

Leo Damore

Leo Damore was born in 1929 in Ontario, Canada, but his family moved shortly thereafter to New York State. He attended Kent State University and graduated with a degree in journalism. In 1969 he was working for the *Cape Cod News* when the incident at Chappaquiddick occurred. After investigating all the reports of the accident, he reportedly received a contract and advance from Random House to write a book about what happened on that fateful night of July 18. The contract, however, was cancelled, supposedly because of pressure from the Kennedy family. His book *Senatorial Privilege: The Chappaquiddick Cover-Up* was eventually published in 1983 by Regnery Gateway. This book is still probably the most investigative and authoritative book about everything that led up to the accident, and the mysterious, unchallenged happenings after the death of Mary Jo Kopechne.

Les Leland had three one-on-one conversations with Damore in 1989, some twenty years after Chappaquiddick. Two of these engagements came during live radio broadcasts on the Connecticut station Les's son Wayne managed. The third meeting came when both were interviewed in New York City on Geraldo Rivera's live TV show, which Leland recalls received the highest ratings ever for that show at the time.

"We discussed privately our theories and thoughts," said Leland. "He talked at length about his interview with Joe Gargan. He mentioned the comic book that was sent to some two million Massachusetts households portraying the Senator as a 'chubby, black sheep, and zeroed in on his history of cheating at Harvard, Virginia traffic violations and Chappaquiddick.'"

Leland recalls that Damore told him Gargan said, "The funny thing about it was, it's all true. He added that one day he wanted the 'real story' of the accident to be told."

Leland went on to say "Leo was impressed with my interview with Maury Povich on *A Current Affair* during this time frame.

"In September or October of 1990, I received a call from Leo. He sounded depressed, to say the least. He was destitute. He had lost everything due to lawsuits and a recent divorce. He had no money and no place to stay. He pleaded with me to stay at my home. I felt very sorry for Leo and saddened by his plight, but my future wife and her two children had just moved into my home.

"I didn't feel obligated or comfortable to invite Leo to live at my home. I really only had met him on those three occasions. Certainly, I felt sympathy for him. But my situation didn't allow me to take him in.

"That was the last time I heard from Leo. I continually thought about him and wished there was something I could have done to help him with his depression. Then I learned he committed suicide in October of 1995."

CHAPTER 24

MANY YEARS LATER

The incident at Chappaquiddick continued to invoke thoughts of injustice to Leland through all the years that had passed. It was an experience he could never stop thinking about.

In mid-September of 2006, he met a judge at the courthouse.

"When I was introduced to him, I told him I had been foreman of the grand jury for the Chappaquiddick accident. He did not know this. During our conversation, I provided some information to him about what had happened during our attempted investigation. I related the story of what had happened on the front steps of the courthouse, when I was warned that Judge Paquet was considering charging me with contempt.

"I mentioned the charge that the judge had given the jury concerning secrecy forever. I also related that both the judge and District Attorney Dinis refused to allow us to subpoena any of the people who had attended the party at the Lawrence cottage that fateful night, or any witnesses who had testified at the inquest.

"Then, I told him about my experience walking into the judge's chamber to request a copy of the impounded inquest transcripts. I explained that I was intimidated at the entire proceeding.

"This judge, who I had just met, had a shocked look on his face, and said, 'That was not only intimidation, that was tampering with the grand jury.' He was visibly shocked and appalled.

"I have talked in the past with another judge, and he, too, had similar comments. A number of lawyers had had the same reaction. They all question the charge by Judge Paquet that our lips are forever sealed.

"In September, 1969, I met with Jack Melemey, who introduced himself as a lawyer from New York City and a member of the New York City Athletic Club. He was extremely interested in the Chappy case. We discussed the rights of the grand jury. Its right to subpoena <u>anyone</u>. Its right to see inquest transcripts. He even explained the runaway grand jury to me. It was evident that he was aware of the DA's actions towards me. Again, the grand jury was the last stumbling block for the Senator to avoid or control."

Another interesting experience Les Leland had was his conversation with Joe Whittemore. James Reston, an editorial writer for the *New York Times* and owner of the *Vineyard Gazette*, had been given copies of the tapes that Leland had recorded for Nancy Hamilton, who was Katherine Cornell's personal assistant.

"When the tapes were returned," Leland related, "they had been basically recorded over, that is, erased. Fortunately, Nancy had made copies and retained the originals. Upon her death, Joe was executor of the estate. The last time he saw the tapes was in the drawer of his desk in his New York City apartment. He left the apartment for several hours, and when he returned found a burglary had taken place. Missing were the tapes, his new word processor typewriter with memory, and a suitcase … probably to put the stolen items in. Another unusual coincidence."

CHAPTER 25

DECIDE FOR YOURSELF

Let the reader be the jury and consider everything we have presented.

There is no doubt, and we have covered this sufficiently, that the Senator did not turn onto the dirt road by accident. The paved road banks to the left. There is a reflecting sign indicating the bank to the left. Dike Road is somewhat covered by bushes. And why would you be driving down a paved road at 7 or 8 miles per hour if you weren't looking for something? Why would you then speed up to 20 miles per hour, or more, when you hit the dirt road?

Why would a girl leave her purse at the cottage, if she was going to the ferry to leave the island and return to her motel for the evening?

Wouldn't it be normal behavior for a girl to tell her friends, or at least one of them, that she is leaving for the evening and returning to her motel … rather than just leaving without notice? Especially since her roommate had the key to the room.

Why didn't the Senator stop at the cottages with lights on near the scene, or the fire station and call for immediate assistance? Such a call possibly would have saved the girl's life.

Why would Christopher "Huck" Look testify that he saw a big, dark colored car with numbers that matched the Senator's license plate if he didn't?

149

What did Joe Gargan and Paul Markham do from approximately 1:15 a.m., when they left the ferry landing, and 2:15 a.m., when they returned to the cottage?

If the Senator's story is true, why did the ferry captain wait at the landing until 12:45 a.m., and spend another half hour tidying up? The fact is, the ferry was always on call.

Why would someone, or some group of people, threaten the life of the foreman of the grand jury and his family if the story and facts were accurate? Also, why threaten the life of John Farrar?

If there was so little drinking at the party, why was so much alcohol purchased, and why were so many empty bottles found after the cottage was vacated?

Chief Dominic Arena said that the driver would have taken a very hard blow to the head, because the windshield on the driver's side was badly smashed in. He couldn't reconcile Kennedy's appearance the next morning with the driver of a car in such an accident.

In his statement to the police, why didn't Kennedy mention the party at the cottage, or the fact that Gargan and Markham went to the pond to try to save the girl?

Massachusetts law clearly states that a "person who wantonly, or in a reckless or grossly negligent manner, did that which resulted in the death of a human being, was guilty of manslaughter, although he did not contemplate such a result." Why, then, wasn't this the charge against the Senator, rather than leaving the scene of an accident?

Why didn't Judge Boyle's findings after the inquest lead to an indictment, or at least further investigation by the grand jury? Because Judge Paquet and District Attorney Dinis blocked all efforts of the grand jury to get to the truth.

The list could go on and on. The questions still remain. Some of the people involved have recanted their positions of that time.

George Killen, then a state police detective lieutenant (and chief of a never-revealed investigation) is quoted in Leo Damore's book as saying that failure to bring that case to a satisfactory resolution was "the biggest mistake" of a long and distinguished police career. Prior to his death, Killen has been quoted as saying that Senator Kennedy "killed that girl the same as if he put a gun to her head and pulled the trigger."

District Attorney Edmund Dinis: "There's no question in my mind that the grand jury would have brought an indictment against Ted Kennedy for manslaughter, if I had given them the case."

Many years have passed and we know one thing for certain: only Senator Edward Moore (Ted) Kennedy really knows what happened that summer evening in 1969. It's questionable if the rest of us will ever know.

He was truthful in his TV speech when he said his failure to report the accident immediately was indefensible. But his behavior, his demeanor, his conduct, —they, too, were all indefensible.

Chappaquiddick has not left the hearts and minds of people worldwide for the past forty years. It will continue to remain an American tragedy until we know the truth about what really happened that tragic night of July 18, 1969.

CPSIA information can be obtained at www.ICGtesting.com
Printed in the USA
LVOW08*1418200114

370181LV00001B/1/P